Arthur William Crichton

A Naturalist's Ramble to the Orcades

Arthur William Crichton

A Naturalist's Ramble to the Orcades

ISBN/EAN: 9783337026592

Printed in Europe, USA, Canada, Australia, Japan

Cover: Foto ©ninafisch / pixelio.de

More available books at **www.hansebooks.com**

SHORT EARED OWL & YOUNG

A NATURALIST'S RAMBLE

TO

THE ORCADES.

BY

A. W. CRICHTON, B.A., F.L.S., F.Z.S.,

MEMBER OF BRITISH ORNITHOLOGISTS' UNION.

LONDON:
JOHN VAN VOORST, 1, PATERNOSTER ROW.

1866.

PREFACE.

THE following chapters contain the unpretending record of a short summer tour made by myself to the Orkney Islands in the months of May and June, 1860, under a youthful desire of becoming practically acquainted with their Natural History, and with a view of obtaining "specimens" for my private collection. They shortly afterwards made their appearance, at various intervals, in the columns of the 'Field' newspaper; and their republication having been urgently solicited by several private friends, I am enabled, by the kind permission of the Editor of that journal, to offer them in their present form to the indulgence of the public.

I am grateful, also, for the opportunity thus afforded me of expressing my acknowledgments to my friends, Mr. Scarth of Bin Scarth, and Mr. Watt of Skael, for so kindly facilitating my exertions during my stay; and to Mr. Joseph Dunn, of Stromness, for his personal assistance and attention.

Throughout these pages I have strictly adhered to Mr. Yarrell's nomenclature of our British Birds.

A. W. C.

February 7th, 1866.

Ornithological Rambles.

CHAPTER I.

> "Oh, Caledonia! stern and wild,
> Meet nurse for a poetic child!
> Land of brown heath and shaggy wood,
> Land of the mountain and the flood."
> *Lay of the Last Minstrel.*

HAVING exhausted all reasonable endeavours to obtain the companionship of some friend during my projected tour, I left London and its "season" by the 9 a.m. train from King's-cross on the brilliant sunshiny morning of the 21st May, 1860. My hopes and anticipations of enjoyment were sanguinely cherished; and if I laboured under any undue apprehensions as to the time that must elapse ere, in my impatience to reach the far North, the intervening distance could be traversed, they were practically annihilated by the ease and velocity with which my train sped along its metal conductors towards its destination, and which, from being comfortably seated in the "coupé," or glass-fronted carriage, I was the more easily enabled to observe.

In the course of the following rude narrative it will be my intention simply to note down unostentatiously the results of my personal experience as an ardent lover of the works of Nature, both by flood and field, in the indulgence of a long-cherished desire of observing the habits and breeding localities of many of our rarer feathered denizens; to enjoy the bold grandeur of their almost inaccessible haunts; and to endeavour to obtain individual specimens, as contributions to a private collection which I have of late years been attempting to form. Nor need I weary my readers by unnecessary detail, inasmuch as a great portion of the ground to which I am now directing my steps has been so ably described, and its natural objects so interestingly sketched, by that eminent sportsman and naturalist Charles St. John, the perusal of whose charming work, 'A Tour in Sutherlandshire by Charles St. John, deceased," has tended so materially to enliven and augment the pleasure of my present excursion.

My train reached Glasgow very punctually to its appointed hour the same evening, and I here took up my quarters for the night.

It was a glorious bright spring morning as the gallant 'Iona,' one of the best steam-ships of the Hutcheson Company, left the quay, and steamed down the Clyde. As we rounded the point of land upon which Roseneath Castle is situated, it was evident, from the few isolated patches that met the eye on the summits of the neighbouring hills, that the snow was still lying thick and unmelted upon the mountains of the more northern Highlands. This I soon discovered to be the case. The view up Loch Fine was new to me, and the effect was exceedingly picturesque.

While proceeding along the Crinan Canal, I heard the well-known cry of the corncrake for the first time this season, and, while steaming up towards Oban, I observed three or four rock-pigeons, and shortly after a tolerably large flight of puffins. At eight o'clock in the evening I reached Banavie, at the commencement of the Caledonian Canal—a capital inn—and on returning from a walk I was delighted to find two large salmon lying in the hall, one of which weighed 33 lbs. and the other 14 lbs.; the former a most magnificent fish, in the primest condition, extremely clean and fresh run. They had both been taken with the fly in the river Lockey, about five miles from the inn—the capturer's first day's sport. Not a bad commencement!

The scenery around here, on this occasion, offered a most dismal and wintry appearance. The ever snow-clad summit of Ben Nevis towered above the surrounding mountains, all of which had their white dresses extending as low as they might be expected to do at a much earlier period of the season.

On the morning of the 25th I proceeded up the Caledonian. I have hitherto never been further north than this point. The effect as we entered Loch Lochay was exceedingly grand; and the swirl of its limpid waters, caused by the progress of the vessel, was all that broke the placid stillness. The rain had ceased for a while, and the long fleecy clouds that rested upon the mountain-tops were beautifully reflected in the water below. At Fort Augustus, where the steamer remains three-quarters of an hour on account of having to pass through the lochs, the famed Gordon Cumming, the African lion-hunter, had erected his museum. This I visited in common with several of the passengers, and inspected his trophies of the chase. Mr. Cumming received me with much cordiality, and paid every attention to my inquiries. He took a great interest in my present tour, and was good enough to show me his collection of eggs, each of which was specially chosen on account of its peculiar markings or brilliant colour. The eggs of the eagles and hawks were very perfect and beautiful specimens, while those of the razor-bill and guillemot would have elicited the admiration of the most distinterested spectator. The well-known variety that exists in the eggs of these birds, not only in the blotches or streaks upon individual eggs, but also in the general or ground colour of the eggs themselves, was beautifully exemplified in the present specimens. The above collection is not usually shown to strangers, as the exposure to the light which their exhibition would involve would be fatal to their retention of colour.

We now entered Loch Ness. A steady fall of rain between this point and Inverness sadly obscured the beauties of the loch. Glen Urquhart, with the remains of its fine old castle, is a lovely spot, and does not fail to arrest the attention.

Arrived at Inverness, I took up my quarters at the Caledonian Hotel. The same evening, while enjoying a walk along the river Ness, I had an opportunity of closely observing a summer snipe, or dunlin (*Tringa variabilis*), as he rested upon a stone upon the water's edge. This was the second bird of the kind I had noticed that day. The following morning, in extending my rambles along the shore, I found the nest of the common yellowhammer (*Emberiza citrinella*), containing four eggs; previous to which I had the inexpressible delight of observing, for the first time, what I believe to have been an osprey or fishing eagle (*Falco haliæetus*) circling in majestic flight far out at sea, until I lost sight of him entirely.

> ". . . There was an air of scorn
> In all his movements, whether he threw round
> His crested head to look behind him, or
> Lay vertical and sportively display'd

> The inside whiteness of his wing declined,
> In gyres and undulations full of grace,
> An object beautifying Heaven itself."
>
> CAMPBELL's *Dead Eagle.*

At 3 o'clock, p.m., the 'Defiance' mail omnibus brought me to Tain, on the Firth of Dornock, along a pretty road skirting the Beauly river and the Firth of Cromarty, a journey of five hours. On all sides I heard that the winter had been unusually severe, and of long continuance throughout Scotland; in fact, that they had had no spring. Nevertheless, vegetation was by no means backward, as Nature seemed to have regained her balance by a sudden and remarkable effort.

There was a vast number of corncrakes (*Gallinula crex*) in the wheat fields along this coast, and on Sunday evening, while taking a walk about two miles from the town, I had the satisfaction of seeing one of these elegant little birds in the act of giving utterance to its discordant cry upon a piece of bare stony ground within a few feet of the road. I am not at all surprised to hear that countless flocks of wild fowl assemble in this bay in the winter season. Admirably protected from the north and west, it would afford plenty of food and harbour to almost any number when driven from the inclement north to seek the shelter of our shores. There would be capital fun here with a punt gun, and thousands are annually slain for the London markets.

The long light nights, even at this point, are exceedingly striking to a stranger from the south, and in another month's time would be much more so. At 11.10 p.m., on May 27, I could see to write quite clearly in the open air. There was a very remarkable change in the weather in the morning. A very bitter cold wind set in from the north-east, chilling to the very marrow, and accompanied with heavy and frequent hail-showers. The same cold, but in a slightly milder form, prevailed next day (May 28th), and I afterwards heard that a fearful gale had been experienced upon the west coast, the effects of which were more or less felt throughout the kingdom; while, curious to relate, in the Shetland Isles, as a traveller informed me, the air was completely unruffled, and a perfect calm reigned throughout. Truly the laws that regulate the distribution of the aërial currents are very puzzling and wonderful! My anticipations of fine and more seasonable weather were necessarily, for the time, very decidedly damped, and though thickly and warmly clad, and amply provided against all reasonable transitions of temperature, it was impossible to be insensible to the bitter fluctuations of its freezing, vehement, and almost arctic gusts.

On the following morning (May 29) the wind suddenly veered round to the south, and remained in that quarter throughout the day, accompanied with a very slight, warm rain, and the change induced by its genial influence was peculiarly refreshing and grateful.

> " Jam veris comites quæ mare temperant
> Impellunt animæ lintea Thraciæ;
> Jam nec prata rigent nec fluvii strepunt
> Hiberna nive turgidi."—Hor.

Never does the serenity and beauty of fair weather more completely recommend itself to the senses than when a sudden and unexpected condition of the same succeeds a prolonged continuance of tempestuous and elementine war.

The state of my health having detained me indoors for many consecutive hours, I loaded my gun as the day declined, and wandered in the calm of the soft light evening, following the road that winds for some four miles along the rough pebbly shore of this very picturesque marine inlet. As the distance between the old town and myself became visibly prolonged, and the wilder and more unfrequented portions of the route were, at every successive step, and round each gently winding slope, more spaciously developed and exposed to view, the lazy tide just hesitating at the lowest ebb, the gleaming masses of broad red seaweed floating like ribbons on the placid water, the partridges calling on the uplands, the oriental softness of the atmosphere, coupled with the excessive stillness of all surrounding nature, contributed to form a scene, the peculiar and surpassing beauty of which it would not be easy to describe.

The rosy tints of sunset chequered the broad arc of heaven, and melted in the bluer distance into bannerets of liquid gold. Many a graceful tern (*Sterna hirundo*) was sailing along, hovering and fishing for its evening meal; the sundry sullen-visaged rooks were stealthily steering homewards to a vast colonial establishment which they have constructed unmolested in the woods to the left of Dunrobin Castle, and a low, smothered, flute-like cry from many a member of the wader tribe some distance further up the creek invited my attention to the spot. Having kept the course of the beaten highway for some three miles and a half, I struck off across a greener portion of the country, where the spring corn, having received a satisfactory fillip from the late humid weather, was doing its utmost to put on a respectable appearance, notwithstanding the unprolific nature of its sandy and uncongenial subsoil. Proceeding steadily in the direction of the sound, I found myself upon a point of land which, jutting out some distance into the stream, formed upon its inner side a small but secluded bay, the nocturnal undisturbed resort of several species of waterfowl. All at once I was aroused by a clamour above my head, emanating from a flock of terns, or sea-swallows, all of whom were thus expressing their unqualified indignation at the impropriety of my visit at this unseasonable and unlooked-for hour. I killed a couple of these birds, each of them being winged by the shot, and offering, ere finally disposed of, a very determined and pugnacious resistance. Having loaded for the second time, I pressed on beyond a low sandy brow still nearer to the water, the undischarged barrel of my piece containing a green cartridge, in case a more distant object should irremediably present itself. At this moment, careering at a great height, there passed an amazing flight of oystercatchers (*Hæmatopus ostralegus*), the nature of the birds being at once evident from the speed with which they cut the air, carrying their long pointed mandibles straight before them, in a direct line with the centre of their bodies, and giving utterance, one and all, to a sustained, high-pitched, piping note, almost amounting to a shake. They were, to all intents and purposes, considerably beyond the reach of an ordinary charge; but, singling out my bird, I fired my cartridge-barrel just as the main body, in the act of a most rapid sweep, were commencing their passage to the opposite shore. Owing to the smoke which hung upon the still air, I entirely lost sight of my particular victim in the *melée*. The whole flock continued its course in unbroken phalanx, nor could I notice any perceptible change in the deportment of a single individual member.

Keeping my eyes unmistakably rivetted upon them as they became

"Small by degrees, and beautifully less,"

I remarked with delight that one of their number slowly and very gradually abandoned the ranks and continued in a course of its own, and at an altitude considerably lower than that of the main body. Sinking in its flight by easy and deliberate gradations, and oscillating in a very undecided manner, it exhibited marked tokens of having been severely hit, and of increasing each moment its indisputably enfeebled state. This continued for some moments longer, when it suddenly dropped, falling into the water in the midst of a luxuriant growth of seaweed, far out upon the bosom of the creek. Having marked the spot to the best of my ability, I had nothing for it but to wade, which I accordingly did, and found my bird most neatly killed, without a speck of blood to soil the plumage, which was perfectly matured and in excellent condition. As some illustration of the brilliance of the long light evenings at this point, I may mention that the above scene took place at 10.40 p.m.

It must not be supposed, because this bird is so named, that its entire food is restricted to its bivalve diet, as many kinds of Crustaceæ and small marine insects are found in its crop. They are exceedingly shy and wary on all occasions, and I only obtained one other specimen in the whole course of my tour. I now killed a little dunlin (*Tringa variabilis*), and, as the shades of night were swiftly closing in, I at once turned back upon my journey homewards, feeling I had some distance to retrace.

The reed-like call of the landrail smote the ear incessantly from the denser covert of the corn and young hay-grass, and the dear little sedge warbler (*Sylvia phragmitis*), hymning its melodies on the midnight air, sweetly serenaded me at every step as I wandered homewards to my own repose.

CHAPTER II.

"For now in our trim boats of Noroway deal,
 We must dance on the waves with the porpoise and seal;
 The breeze it shall pipe, so it pipe not too high,
 And the gull be our songstress whene'er she flits by."
   Claud Halcro's Norse ditty.—"PIRATE."

IT was my intention to make a stay of some days, if weather had demanded it, in this town, as I was anxious to make a short incursion against the seals which occasionally frequent the neighbourhood of the sand-banks and shoals which are visible at low water about the mouth of the Firth, and around which the various fish upon which they feed congregate in great numbers in the currents and shallows of the narrow places. These, to my mind, beautiful but peculiar instances of vertebrate animals are yearly becoming more scarce upon the shores of Scotland.

In days gone by, the *Phoca*, or seal, was as familiar and well known to every dweller on the coast as their own watchdog or the birds of the air; and the various time-honoured legends and nursery stories connected with these monsters of the deep, and some of which are so ably interwoven by Sir Walter Scott in his admirable works of fiction, point them out as having been most constant frequenters of the numerous rocky inlets of the North, before the encroaching progress of civilisation had began to scare them from the haunts of men.

The following tradition has been prevalent for the last two hundred years or more in all the districts where these animals abound. There exists an indigenous feeling in the breasts of the fishermen that every seal is the earthly embodiment of a condemned antediluvian spirit, and that once in seven years it casts its skin, and resuming, for the nonce, its original bodily shape, fills and carries on its position and calling in the scale of human society. Whoever, under these circumstances, becomes the fortunate possessor of the skin thus cast aside, maintains, for the time being, the most complete control over the actions and intentions of its original proprietor. Now, it so happened that a poor fisherman perceived, during one of his coastal rambles, a number of youthful female forms, of surpassing beauty and grace, disporting themselves in the glassy wavelets of a placid and sequestered bay. A short time afterwards he discovered a seal-skin of unusual beauty, carefully rolled up upon a ledge of rock in this same bay. Securing the prize, he carried it away and concealed it; but he had no sooner entered his threshold than, seated in silence, unclad and alone, he beheld an exquisitely lovely woman, wringing her hands in distress, and loudly lamenting that, having lost her sea-dress, she must remain for ever on the earth. Having provided her with suitable habiliments, he wooed and won her for his wife; and many a year rolled rapidly away, a witness of their united affection and peaceable contentment. But—" the course of true love never did run smooth;" and it came to pass that on one fine morning the fair merlady discovered her long-lost garb, and, before her bewildered husband could essay to prevent her, had gained the margin of the boiling ocean, and, gracefully waving her pendant fin, bounded into the surge with a farewell whisk of her tail, and rejoined her seal-husband in the depths below.

The old seals come into the shallows at this time of year for the purpose of calving; and the young seals, closely following the mother in the open sea, exuberant and free, and affording full scope for their curious evolutions and playful gambols, offer to the lover of young animals a very attractive domestic episode. They are often caught and made great pets of by their captors, and the following anecdote offers a striking instance of their singular affection and attachment :—

A poor fisherman's family had long possessed one of these animals, which they had brought up from infancy, and which, by its lamb-like innocence and amusing antics, afforded an unceasing source of gratification and pleasure. Sickness at last invaded their quiet home, and one of the youthful members of the family was apparently fast sinking under the baleful effects of some unintelligible disease. As is often the case under these circumstances, the auguries and revelations of a seer or wise woman, and the existence of one or two of which mysterious personages these outlandish neighbourhoods are often proud to boast, were gravely consulted by the desponding parents. She at once decided that, so long as the malignant influence was suffered to infest the premises, no beneficial change could possibly be expected to ensue. The poor little *Phoca* was accordingly carried some three or four days' voyage out to sea, and was then consigned, with much malediction and disgrace, to the unfostering strangeness of its native element. Some forty-eight hours afterwards, and in the dead of night, a low moaning sound * outside the cabin door, alternating between a languid grunt and a more plaintive bark, roused the terror-stricken inmates from their sleep, and filled them with abject sensations of ghostly misgiving and dread. On opening the casement the rejected little favourite was seen, toilworn and weary, bespeaking admittance in its child-like accents to its usual shelter and repose. Again the now-dreaded

* The cry of the seal is wild and mournful, difficult to describe, but something between the mew of a cat and the howl of a dog; a most unpleasant sound it is, though it sometimes harmonizes sufficiently well with the wild scenery surrounding them.—*St. John's Tour in Sutherland.*

little animal was subjected to a still more lengthened voyage, after having been first mutilated in the most shameful and barbarous manner. Its expressive little eyeballs were ruthlessly branded out by wires, made red hot for the purpose, and it was for a second time cast overboard with every sign of contumelious disgrace. Again, also, in the still midnight hour, that same plaintive voice more piercingly echoed on the stilly air. The faithful little creature had dragged its famished and suffering frame, by an instinct that human ideas are unable to solve, to render up an agonised existence upon the very threshold of its unnatural and cruel guardians.*

There is an individual resident in this town, a carpenter by trade, popularly known by the more spirited appellation of "the seal hunter," a well-knit, active, game little man, who has, many a time and oft, braved the stern dangers of an impetuous sea, and supplied his family, and indirectly his pocket, the long dark winter through, with many a reeking gallon of seal-oil. His assistance having been procured, and his co-operation decided upon, we agreed to take advantage of the first seasonable day, and, being for my

* For a further illustration of my experience of the extraordinary tractability of this animal, see 'Curiosities of Natural History,' Third Series, by Frank Buckland, M.A., vol. ii., p. 258. Richard Bentley, New Burlington Street. 1866.

own part desirous of hastening my journey northwards, I determined to abide by its chances of success.

For two whole days I was unable to venture on the briny sea, but at last a favourable breeze prevails, and I ordered his boat to be got ready, and equipped myself for a start. My small pea-rifle, recently built by Mr. Beattie, of Regent-street, and a more ancient distance-killing gun, by Smith, of Princes-street, were the weapons chosen for this occasion.

On descending together to the water's edge, my eyes at once rested upon a trim-built sailing-boat, the joint construction of himself and his father, moored far out in the tidal current in a bend of the creek of the Kyle of Dornoch. In order to effect an embarkation it was necessary to wade out a very long distance, as the creek is extremely shallow at this point, and her draught of water completely precluded her being able to be brought up any nearer to the drier portion of the shore. It would also have been equally impossible to have made use of a boat for the purpose, had any such been at hand, so slight was the inclination of its sandy bed at this portion of the inlet.

Taking advantage of Mackenzie's shoulders (for that was the gallant seal-hunter's family designation), I reached the boat dry-footed and secure; and having disposed my artillery in the most offensive, but at the same time commodious, form, our sails were hoisted, and we were quickly under weigh and making steady progress to the more open water. The sun was shining its very best,—the wind blew soft and warm,—the whole landscape, as we steered away, glistened more and more with all the slight transitions of continuous changing light which a bold and mountainous background is so adapted to reflect; and all the surrounding scene revelled in the rich accompaniments of a brilliant and propitious day. Onward the little vessel pursued its way, which we beguiled with many a tale of ocean marvel and provincial legend, as in our lengthened tacks we glided gaily over the blue water.

We had passed several patches of sand and shingle, just visible above water in the present state of the tide, and more or less tenanted by oystercatchers, terns, and several species of the commoner varieties of gull, when a long, smooth, flat sand-bank faintly loomed ahead, darkly verging on the far horizon. Some twenty minutes later, when we had made considerable way, Mackenzie softly hinted that seals might possibly be found upon this bank, and that he fancied he detected them with the naked eye. I raised my glass and swept the distant view, and then brought it steadily to bear upon the spot. Great indeed was my surprise and pleasure as I descried, for the first time in my life, from a dozen to fifteen of these most curious creatures.

As we drew nearer to the spot, the scene became

every moment more intensely exciting, not to say amusing, to behold. Varying very materially in size, from six and seven feet long down to three or four, they appeared to be of two kinds.* Some, stretched out upon the bare dry sand, were basking, motionless, in evident repose; while others were performing the very drollest antics, pursuing one another in playful mood— propelling their unwieldy bodies in a sort of snake-like manner, with a peculiar undulatory movement of the tail, their shining forms flashing in the clear sunlight as they disported themselves in gleesome merriment on the warm dry sand. Some, gliding off the bank, dived invisibly away; while others, reappearing from the element at different points, went shuffling along at the edge of the water. As I grasped my rifle with the eagerness of hope, the seal-hunter gravely hinted that our best precautions would be as unavailing as my own aspirations, as the seals upon this bank were always extremely wild, being so often scared by the passage to and fro of vessels in the Firth. And true enough; for as our nearer approach seemed at first to increase at once the life, the interest, and the reality of the scene, and these extraordinary animals loomed more distinctly upon the sight, they all at once, as though the act was preconcerted, in the twinkling of an eye,

---

* The common seal (*Phoca vitulina*), and the Greenland or harp seal (*P. Greenlandica*).

scuttled simultaneously into the water, where, with a violent splashing and vexatious turmoil, they vanished from the sight. Here and there, at various points a vast distance off, they exhibited for a moment their round black heads, resembling in a great degree the larger cannon-shot which, in naval practice, seem to rest for a moment on the surface of the water ere they finally disappear. We steered along the edge of the bank, which now lay exposed like the back of some huge monster of the deep, bare and naked in the scorching sun; and the death-like stillness of the scene contrasted strangely with its recent animation and enlivenment. Occasionally one would raise its head, but at a distance that only ball could reach, and, whenever I fired, almost before the ball could strike the water, would instantaneously vanish in a cloud of spray. We now bore away towards the mouth of the Firth, making for a bank of larger extent, about two miles off the point of Tarbet Ness. Wherever a point of dry sand came into sight, there would seals be lying—the gulls quietly feeding amongst them in the truest spirit of fraternisation, in greater or smaller numbers; but, ever on the alert, they were off into the deep long before it was in my power to commence offensive operations.

It was very amusing to scour the distant water with attentive gaze as one or other of us imparted the intelligence in an under tone, "that one of these animals had come up to breathe." We would sometimes continue sailing smoothly on, for half-an-hour or more, without the smallest semblance of any living object to vary the monotony of the scene. Sometimes, at a moment the least expected, the sable head of some enormous monster would suddenly appear within apparent range, and the immediate seizure of gun or rifle would sadly disconcert the quiet imbibition of a dram of whiskey, or the calm discussion of a biscuit. By and by we passed a long, low, corrugated shoal, on the further side of which I could plainly distinguish two seals. On this I landed, and attempted to stalk them, but without avail. I had but the mortification of observing their reproachful countenances gleaming far out on the smooth water on the sheltered side. It is most surprising the distance they can dive on end without coming up for air; and when they do appear, their smooth, round, innocent-looking heads, slightly spheroidal in form, look somewhat like those of infant children of the coloured race of man, nimbly resting on the wave.

Most wonderful and beautiful is the manner in which these creatures are adapted to the purposes which they are intended to serve. No person who has ever seen one of them close at hand can have failed to have noticed their very expressive and strikingly developed eye. "The eye of the seal is fitted for a double action—for seeing either in the water or the air. There is no eye which can be said to have, upon the whole, to perform these offices so effectually. They have to use their eyes deep in the water, when there is very little light, or, indeed, none; the water being sometimes frozen over, aud a deep stratum of snow lying upon the ice." Awkward as the seal is upon land, I cannot imagine an animal whose motions in the water are attended with more graceful ease. We are all aware of the extreme velocity with which fish are able to cleave their native element; but an animal whose province is to feed upon them in its turn, must necessarily be provided with still more remarkable powers. These the seal possesses to an amazing degree; and the extraordinary agility with which it can alter its direction in an instant, and accommodate itself in every possible motion and position, must be seen to be believed. It is also interesting to observe the way in which the seal opens and closes its nostrils in rapid succession while in the act of taking breath. "The natural state of the nostrils is to remain closed, and an effort is required to open them when the seal reaches the air." A continuous and amusing change of expression is induced upon the creature's countenance by this act,' while the long bristling feelers, which must be most useful in exploring the irregular surfaces of icebergs under water, curl stiffly backwards *à la militaire*, and impart an air of considerable sedateness to the whole contour.

But I am digressing. Pushing onwards to the

larger sandbank, where we had counted on a perfect exhibition and considerable sport, we were both to experience a grevious disappointment, for on the present occasion there was not a single seal upon it.

Previous, however, to this discovery, and while we were both engaged in loud and listless conversation, some five-and-thirty yards behind us suddenly uprose the head and shoulders (if I may so term them) of a tremendous seal. Like Arethusa—

"Prospiciens, summa flavum caput extulit unda."

My gun was lying upon the stern-sheets ready cocked, and loaded with green cartridge; but with a sort of feeling that a specimen marked with the blemish of a single ball would be more acceptable than a trophy that was riddled with shot, I raised my rifle and fired; but the lurching and rolling of the boat made it most difficult to take a steady aim, and (shall I confess it?) I missed it.

With a terrible consternation of the element, as it took its leave of the upper air, and a few moments of private remorse, all things resumed their original serenity.

It was getting late in the afternoon, and as the flood-tide had now commenced to run, we put the helm a-port and started upon our voyage home. I feel certain that I was extremely foolish, on the present occasion, to make such constant use of the rifle, since opportunities thus trifled with would have been more favourably seized had I used the gun. For so precarious are the chances with ball,—unless the sea is very smooth and the boat is steady, and you are pretty confident in your own powers and those of your weapon,—and so deadly is the execution of the shot-charge when brought to bear within a reasonable range, that the latter weapon, on ordinary occasions, is decidedly to be preferred.

Nothing of interest or event occurred in the course of our homeward sail. We both felt that a more unimpeachable day will not be witnessed among all that may adorn the circle of the year; and I could not but feel grateful that supreme enjoyment had prevailed throughout a health-giving though an unsuccessful day.

CHAPTER III.

> "Harold was born where restless seas
> Howl round the storm-swept Orcades."
> *Lay of Last Minstrel.*

I LEFT Tain on the 2nd of June by the mail which takes its departure at ten minutes after one A. M., and arrived at Wick the same evening.

The keen morning air was intensely still; and when the appropriate silence was occasionally broken by one or two shrill calls upon the guard's long trumpet, its sharp decisive tones awoke the little dunlins and sand-pipers, who feebly responded to its distant echoes with their peculiar whistling kind of note.

For the next fifteen or twenty miles our route was very beautiful, and at one point of the road, where it rounded the scarp of a grassy declivity, two noble stags peered at us for a moment from the brow above, and then bounded off into the thicket. Occasionally, and as the scenery becomes more heathery and bare, the blue mountain hares steal amongst the herbage, canter fox-like along the slope, and disappear beyond the brow. We still bowl on; the sun is bright, but the wind is cold, and here and there a parcel of the Royston or hooded crow (*Corvus cornix*) are busily employed in collecting their matutinal meal of grubs and worms, or foraging for carrion or eggs to feed their callow brood. A few more weary miles, and we enter the town of Wick. This is a seaport, so fragrant of fish, that Miss Sinclair observes * "that when she entered it she thought of her brother's voyage in a herring smack, when the seats were barrels of herrings, and the staircase from the cabin formed by piles of casks." It is the great emporium of the north Scotch fisheries, and supports no less than fourteen hundred fishing boats, each of which is manned by at least seven men, so that some idea may be formed of the busy scenes that are enacted, and the general activity that prevails here in the fishing-season. The population is consequently very large, and as this sea is peculiarly dangerous at times, numerous are the tales of death and misery which each season contributes to the page of time. The men are intensely bronzed by the cutting sea blast, and the women appeared to me to grow wrinkled and careworn at an early age. At 11.30 on the morning of the 1st of June, I mounted the coach for its last northern stage across the north west corner of Caithness. For the first few miles, although the surrounding country is completely denuded of trees and vegetation, except such scanty herbage as serves to offer an equivocal subsistence to

* 'Shetland and the Shetlanders,' by Catherine Sinclair. 1840.

a few scattered sheep, yet the hedge on each side of the road, and which is composed of beech and quickset judiciously combined, thrives so wonderfully notwithstanding its very exposed situation, that it remains for a long distance the only object of interest. An ill-starred cuckoo tried in vain to find a tree to perch upon, and rested in despair upon the hedges. All around is surprisingly flat, and more especially as compared to the bolder inequalities of Sutherlandshire.

At last the road makes a slight *détour* from its systematic straightness, and we suddenly arrive at the top of a gentle declivity, and a panorama breaks upon the view with all the effect which non-expectation contributes to enhance. Stretched below the horses' feet extend the slated roofs and ornate spires of houses and churches. Straight before us, a narrow sheet of, on this occasion, smooth sea distinguishes the fair island of Orkney, which looms in the background of our picture from the mainland. To the left, the houses and streets shelve step by step down to the waterside; while to the right, the flagstone cliffs, precipitous and bleak, of Scotia's northern shore, stretch away in a well-defined semicircle till they end abruptly, as it stands out stereoscopically in the sun's rays, in the bluff and rugged head of Dunnit. Shrilly heralded by an echoing " yard of tin," the leaders straining on the bit, and the ribbons gracefully waved by an old and experienced hand, the Inverness mail, after rounding the foot of the aforesaid incline, and crossing the bridge that spans the river that takes its name from the town, gallantly and merrily bowls into the ancient township of Thurso.

A motley scene is enacting upon the hill above us, and flags and banners of manifold design and mottoes; orderly groups of citizens, from the chief magistrate to the humblest Highland chiel; the Freemasons with their respective badges and orders of brotherhood; the Rifle corps with their bayonets fixed, and band in readiness to strike up at a moment's notice; the drum and bagpipes of some Highland clan ; but, above all, a tripod stand of timber carrying a heavy pulley, with a windlass and a massive block of stone, proclaim the object of the scene. Sir George Sinclair, Bart., of Thurso Castle, is in the act of laying the foundation stone of a new academy which promises to be a great acquisition to the town. In the centre of a dense mass I could just distinguish the bared white head of Sir George, in the act of making his address; and, after a pause of a few moments, three hearty cheers, accompanied by a tattoo from the Highland drummer, denoted its conclusion. A murmur of satisfaction, and three verses of a hymn, and it was then most inspiriting to feel the time marked by the bass drum, as the band struck up the National Anthem and the loyal hearts of Victoria's favoured subjects glowed with enthusiasm even in this distant corner of Britain. The Rifles formed, and the procession marching away, brought this interesting ceremony to a close.

In the course of this afternoon I walked up to the castle, and had the pleasure of finding Sir George at home. He received me with a kindness and hospitality which I shall not easily forget, and many a pleasant hour passed happily away beneath the shadow of his ample rooftree.

The same evening I took a stroll along the heights to the westward. The air was calm and still, and the sea smooth; and as I threaded the edge of the cliffs that stretch away beyond the little village of Scrabster, where his late Majesty once possessed a royal castle, a mingled concert of bird's voices suddenly pervaded the otherwise silent air, and as I neared the spot a countless throng of seafowl were nestling and huddling together upon the turf-mantled summit of a shapeless mass of stone, which was completely isolated from the mainland by a deep and sickening abyss. I could have shot hundreds, but it would have been impossible to obtain one. This was the only spot on this point of the coast on which I found birds congregated to this extent. They had evidently chosen it as affording them the best protection, on account of its insulated position. They seemed perfectly aware of their security, and remained serenely undisturbed at my approach.

Upon a piece of very rough ground, covered with low heaps of shaly fragments, I shot a fine specimen of the turnstone (*Strepsilas interpres*). This was the only instance in which I observed this bird throughout the whole course of my tour.

It produces a species of fearful pleasure to saunter along these airy terraces of nature; the sea unheard below, its motion rendered visible alone by the churning of its whitening waves as you peer beyond their beetling brow.

After a parting survey of the charming view which Thurso Castle so prettily commands, I prepared for progress. A dog cart brought myself and luggage to the quay. Here the Orkney mail steamer was only awaiting the arrival of the post-bags to commence her passage. I was the only passenger on board; the wind was rising, and I made my mind up for a lively sea.

When once under weigh, and well beyond the precincts of the very picturesque bay of Thurso, the murky cliffs of Dunnit Head gradually became the last visible remnant of the mainland of Britain. Later in the afternoon, and well out upon the open sea, my attention was perceptibly drawn to the fact that we were now exposed to the full broad sweep of the Atlantic, mingling its restless waters with the cooler rapids of the Northern Ocean. Here the Frith of the ever dreaded Pentland rolls its boiling current with a force that many a silenced voice could once have testified. Squalls of the most fearful kind often come on here in the winter months; and there are times when the little boat is quite unable to cross. After ploughing through the billows for another hour and a half, we coasted along the lofty crags of Orkney, composed of thin and nearly horizontal layers of brown clay slate, towering upwards to an immense height, and stretching far away on either hand in rigid hard-developed outline. As our tiny vessel steamed proudly beneath these stupendous cliffs, I felt as though I was sailing upon some vast lake, instead of an arm of the mighty ocean; the witness of this still unchanging grandeur, and navigated only by the porpoise and the whale, ages before the first tree had nodded to its fall, or weak, short lived man had taught the giants of the forest

"To cleave the unsettled bosom of the deep,
Or shape his course upon the trackless wave."

Uncrumbled and unstained by time, these mighty monuments have stood a staunch impenetrable barrier against old father Neptune's impetuous advances. There is something extremely dignified in their dusky, dark gamboge hue, fading in the distance into purple indistinctness, and the endless movements of many an ocean bird either descending to the wave on quivering wing, or feathering upward to their final roost, infused a life into the background of the picture.

Like some weird spectre from an earlier world,

standing alone as if to warn or taunt the daring mariner, we passed the famed " Old Man of Hoy" a tall, gaunt pillar of unhewn native rock, uprising from the water to a height of 1180 feet in direct perpendicularity. Its extreme peculiarity causes it to be well known to every sailor in the north, and, had it existed in the Eubœan sea, or on the coast of Samothrace, its praises would not have been unsung in Sapphic stanza, or Pindaric ode.

It has been conjectured that these islands derive their name from the seal—*orc*, in the language of the Northmen, signifying a seal. They formerly belonged to Denmark; and it was in these straits and narrow seas that the chiefs of the Vikingr or Scandinavian pirates made their predatory excursions and committed their unhallowed depredations:

> " For thither came in times afar,
> Stern Lochlin's sons of roving war;
> The Norsemen, trained to spoil and blood,
> Skilled to prepare the raven's food;
> Kings of the main their leaders brave,
> Their barks the dragons of the wave."
> *Lay of the Last Minstrel.*

In 1468 the islands were pawned to Scotland for 50,000 florins, and the pledge has never been redeemed.

At 6.30 P.M. we dropped anchor in the blue harbour

of Stromness. The town is a curious and homogeneous accumulation of small gray houses, piled one above another on the sloping hill, and the nursery of many of our bravest and most experienced sailors. The principal thoroughfare, unpaved and sinuous, is so narrow that in most places it would be impossible for two vehicles to pass, and the bye streets are simply a series of steps and stairs, and each side of which you may generally touch with both hands at a stretch. As I intended taking up my quarters here for the present. I at once engaged my lodgings, which turned out so comfortable, and my landlady, a Mrs. Spence by name, was so attentively solicitous for my welfare, that I most confidently recommend a sojourn under her roof, both as to comfort, economy and position, to any future traveller to this place. On the following morning, a heavy rain having fallen during the night, I sallied forth with my gun, and, free and unfettered as the breeze itself, set out upon my first exploration of the coast.

It is very pleasant to wander forth in the exhilarating morning air, surrounded with scenery as novel as it is exciting. It is pleasant to pursue your morning ramble, uninterrupted by the passing throng, over country "unrailway-ed" and "unvilla-ed." No anxious tourists who have lost their way; no panniered donkeys with their shouting attendants; no slaughtering Cockneys with their rusty artillery harassing every unoffending bird. Nevertheless, even here I observe the rapid progress of cultivation; the deep drainage, the walled fields, and the extending prosperity are contributing their unerring share towards thinning the ranks of the winged visitants of the island.

The coast along which my present walk extends is remarkably varied with rock and shingle, with steep abrupt declivity, and shelving sandy shore. Drying or fermenting upon the rocks, stand great heaps of seaweed, large quantities of which are shipped to Glasgow, Hull, &c., for the manufacture of kelp, from which Glauber salts and other chemical substances are extracted. Fitful gleams of sunshine threaten to disperse the mist, developing during their short existence the rugged outline of the hills of Hoy Island in bold and picturesque perspective.

On rounding a point of rock I saw and shot a female wheatear (*Sylvia œnanthe*), which restless little bird is comparatively common here. They seem particularly fond of the rocks, steep banks, and stone walls of this locality, and they lay a very neatly-shaped, fresh-coloured pale blue egg. They are taken, or used to be taken, in the summer season in great numbers, on our South Downs in the county of Sussex.

Here and there I see a solitary specimen of the lesser black-backed gull (*Larus fuscus*) flying far out of shot along the shore, while o'er the bosom of the emerald ocean flap dark detachments of cormorants or shags, looking for the world like long-necked demons speeding on an errand of death or torment to some imprisoned soul. Steadily onward, let the wind be high or low, like the arrows of remorseless fate, they cleave the unresisting air, until, perceiving some wandering shoal of coalfish or blenny, they halt upon the swelling sea, and, after diving and fishing till their voracious appetite is temporarily appeased, or their craw well provided with fish, resume their unhallowed progress to some favourite rock to digest at leisure their unsavoury feast. A few ducks are to be seen at the entrance of the bay, but most of them are already off to the far north.

I now passed a curious old dilapidated ruin of a church, with a walled churchyard crammed with gravestones and large monuments, and evidently still made use of as a burial ground. A very picturesque little cove runs some way inland, a short distance beyond this point. The rocky nature of the coast ceases for awhile, and a smooth bed of sand at low water tempts a few sea-birds here to feed. There were only a few herring-gulls (*Larus argentatus*)—of which I shot one—upon it as I passed. On my return it was tenanted by oyster-catchers. The latter are far too wary and wild a bird to be approached on ordinary occasions. In the opposite distance, precipitous and grand, majestic Hoy rears its proud and lofty head 1138 feet above the sea; while to the right, and in the direction I am tending, the ever-dreaded Black Craig lifts its rocky summit to the sky. Many are the terrible stories associated with this frightful cliff, and the following I myself heard from several eye-witnesses:—A few years ago, an ill-fated vessel, the Star, of Dundee, after being tossed uncontrollably by the raging sea, was hopelessly driven upon a dreadful-looking block of dark rock at the foot of the craig. Of course she quickly went to pieces, and the unfortunate crew perished, One young man, however, named Henry Johnstone, after struggling ineffectually with the waves, was washed into a hole in the craig, which in the lapse of centuries has evidently been hollowed out by the action of the sea. The bottom part, or floor as it were, of this hollow slopes upwards into the interior of the rock, though its mouth or aperture is completely closed at high tide by every succeeding wave. In this situation he actually existed four days and nights; his sensations for four hours out of the six, when he expected every moment to suffocate, being simply indescribable. As a curious and providential circumstance, there floated to him from the wreck a barrel of herrings, a feather mattress, and a small tin mug. By means of the first he obtained his sustenance. The mattress he cut open and stuffed the feathers into his boots for warmth; and with the mug he caught the water as it dripped from the roof of his cell. Driven to desperation, he at last attempted and actually scaled the craig at a point which it makes the blood run cold to survey. When he appeared in the town, where he was well known, upon a Sunday morning, and sparely clothed, the inhabitants fled before him, supposing him a spectre from the dead. Thanksgivings were offered up in all the churches for his safe deliverance, and all testified by their universal sympathy their astonishment at his marvellous escape.

Being desirous of gaining that point, and thus getting a more extended glimpse of the surrounding scene, I crossed a wide neck of land that, ending in a long low point formed by successive sloping steps of rock, juts out in the tideway, shooting in my progress a common bunting (*Emberiza miliaria*), killing it in a very cleanly manner, without a single speck of blood to soil the feathers. I noticed these birds in great plenty in the young corn, and they are commonly termed the corn bunting in the north of Scotland. I do not think that it is popularly known that one of the specific distinctions of this bird is a curious little palatine knob projecting downwards from the interior surface of its upper mandible, and aptly mentioned by Mr. Yarrell. It is doubtless provided for the purpose of cutting or bruising the seeds upon which it feeds.

Gaining the coast again on the opposite side, I rested upon a very abrupt grassy bank, many feet above the level of the beach. A herring-gull at this moment, suddenly swooping in his flight, came just within range as I dropped him on the rocks below. As he fell perfectly dead upon a dry sloping rock flat upon his back, with his wings extended, I left him there until my return to consolidate and stiffen.

The bank now rises, step by step, upon basaltic perpendicular rock, and as I peered beyond its head a flight of rock pigeons (*Columba livia*) darted from my feet and vanished round a turn of the shore, too suddenly for me to fire. I now crossed two trickling rivulets and a stone wall, and then this bold and rugged cliff shoots upwards from the earth in frowning majesty. It is a considerable strain upon the lungs to reach the top without a rest: the cries of a few gulls sailing in the air far above, increasing as you labour up the ascent in number and intensity, as the news is gradually spread of your unceremonious intrusion upon their places of selected abode.

Just as my head appeared above the topmost brow, my eyes were greeted with a pleasant sight. All the most lofty ledges of this most horrid cliff were the breeding-places of the herring-gull, who tenanted them in surprising numbers; the birds dropping off as I approached, with wings extended on the air, with a grace and unaffected ease, that, if one could only divest one's self of unpleasant associations, was elegant and lovely to behold. Craning for a moment beyond its edge, the dark blue heaving ocean swell was seething on the rocks below—far, far, in dizzy distance.

The smooth, short, sheep-nibbled, slippery turf slopes, for some yards distant, down towards the sudden precipitousness of the craig, so that, with a brisk wind, your footing, in such a situation, becomes unpleasantly uncertain.

On the first undoubted evidence of your unprivileged intrusion, the birds, simultaneously taking flight in myriads and myriads, fill the air around with their wild and multitudinous cries, sailing in whirling circles round your head in a manner that cannot fail to call forth the envy and admiration of a pinionless biped—causing by their intricate and airy evolutions a perceptible dizziness of brain as you peer into regionless space above.

I have repeatedly noticed upon these occasions that these birds never place themselves in such a position that, were you to fire and kill one, he would fall upon the land on which you stand. The whole time that I remained upon this spot, with this vast assemblage of sea-fowl so close and noisy, I could not have shot a single specimen but would have fallen into the sea below; consequently I did not fire at all.

On a subsequent visit to the spot, I found a pair of peregrines (*Falco peregrinus*) breeding in the face of the cliff. Their young were evidently hatched, as the sharp, shrill, *cheep! cheep! cheep!* of the female as she continually disappeared and returned with food, dropping like a stone over the edge of the rock, and her rapid, gliding motions beautifully helmed by her spreading tail, fully tended to confirm. The effect of the sunset upon her wing-coverts and tail-feathers, as she threw over to the light, was very curious and rich, and it is amazing what speed this rare and beautiful falcon can attain:

> "My plumage bears the crimson blush,
> When ocean by the sun is kissed!
> When fades the evening's purple flush,
> My dark wing cleaves the silver mist."
> LONGFELLOW'S *Sea-Diver*.

When I first saw her, she flew within easy shot, but my gun was not loaded; and though I secreted myself carefully in a hollow and waited patiently for her various returns, apparently conscious of my presence, she never again presented herself within range, nor, as I have heard other naturalists remark, did she approach the nest twice in the same direction.

I have been fortunate in being able to obtain a skin, shot here, and Mr. Dunn informs me that he has seen a peregrine flying towards him round the side of a hill, and that he has concealed himself behind the covert of a wall, apparently well posted for a shot; but that as soon as the bird approached almost within range, it caught sight of the muzzle of the gun with its wonderful eye, and immediately shooting upwards, as perpendicularly swift as if fired out of a gun itself, continued its progress far out of harm's reach. At other times, when shooting rock pigeons at the foot of the craig, if any happen to be slightly wounded, but still able to fly, this bird, singling out in a moment the weak straggler from the flock, has, though previously unseen or heard, dropped from her watchful position, and striking the doomed quarry, borne it off swift as thought to her ledge.

Having now made the descent of the craig, and commenced my return homewards, I clambered down a steep bank for a stroll upon the shore. I now shot a small bird, which turned out to be the rock pipit (*Anthus obscurus*). It was resting upon the edge of the highest peak of a crag that overhung the flat range of shelving rocks from which I fired. Instead of toppling over, as I had expected would be the case, it had received the brunt of the charge and fell dead upon the spot on which it stood. There being no visible evidence of any sort of communication, however circuitous, by which the top of the cliff could be reached from the rocks below, I had no choice but to scale its face. This I fortunately succeeded in effecting, though not without that continual misgiving which an inexperienced cragsman may well be expected to entertain. There is something extremely disagreeable in finding yourself perched half-way up a perpendicular height, labouring under a reasonable uncertainty as to whether it is more possible to progress or to retire, the small, protuberating, craggy points, jutting out above your head just sufficiently far to incapicitate you from calculating your distance from the summit; while the scanty indentations that have offered you a precarious footing thus far are so few and far between, that to retrieve your exact steps would be positively out of the question.

Extreme confidence is the secret of this style of climbing. In tree-climbing, on the contrary, the profusion of lateral branches and the natural excrescences where branches have or should have been, afford a reasonable amount of protection in case the hand or foot slips. Here, however, the uneven surface of the rock affords little or no hold, and muscular pressure is the only means of availing yourself of what there is. Not to mention that these few available points which the eye marks out, or the foot agreeably seizes, are, in nine cases out of ten, bleached, weather-worn, or cracked, and are consequently but too likely to cause undue and precipitate retrogression.

Having obtained my bird, which turned out to be a female, and had probably a nest in the vicinity, though I was quite unable to discover it, I set about commencing my descent, which I also successfully accomplished, so far as gaining the original ledge was concerned. Along this I had to pursue my course for some distance before I could reach a more traversable portion of the shore. After a few steps, I did not at first notice that the rocks were covered with an extremely thin coating of marine vegetation in the shape of a yellowish-green sea-weed, the same being kept continually moist by the passage of a trickling spring which issued from a crevice in the solid rock above. My boots, being heavily nailed as a precautionary safeguard when traversing turfy slopes, were doubly treacherous for rock-travelling. My first footsteps, then, over this state of things were thus very naturally succeeded by a fall which sent self, gun, and bird, rolling over, pellmell, in rapid downward course towards the sea. Arrived at the extreme edge of the watery element, my progress was fortunately stayed, as rising somewhat bruised, but more especially concerned as to the welfare of my gun, the bronzing of whose barrels could not be said to be improved by the process, and meeting with no incident of noteworthy remark, I continued my journey homewards.

On the morning of the 5th of June, the wind being too boisterous and the sea too unruly for any kind of aquatic excursion, I determined upon an inland expedition, and accordingly set off in the direction of the Loch of Steanhouse.

Leaving Stromness on the east side, and well provided with No. 4 and No. 8 shot, royal and green cartridges, I pursued my journey, and skirting the extremity of the bay, my road at last diverged in three directions. Taking the centre one, which mounted a heathery and very barren hill, I followed its course till it entered a pretty considerable cutting, and then found myself upon a newly-constructed and one of the best formed roads I ever saw.

Countless numbers of the common plover or peewit (*Vanellus cristatus*) frequent and breed in this portion of the island, and I could have slain hundreds had my intentions been so unwarrantably murderous. After proceeding at a tolerably brisk pace for about two miles and a half, the beautiful and extensive loch suddenly opened before me, and kept increasing in extent of view at every succeeding step. Leaving the road at a point where, by a gradual turn, it began to run parallel to the side of the loch, I traversed some cultivated land that lay between, and continued my progress along the edge of the water.

The sun now burst forth with a brilliancy that was the more welcome after the morose and gusty weather of the preceding days. Great quantities of plover here rose in all directions, and followed me in the most obstinate manner; swooping suddenly in their well-known flapping style of flight, in a manner that tended to completely scare anything I might be anxious to work up to by unusual caution; and keeping up so annoyingly their pertinacious cry, that I shot one out of sheer aggravation, and packed him carefully in my box, with its layers of cotton-wool, as an example to the rest of its species.

This is certainly a very magnificent expanse of water, and must be crowded with wildfowl in the winter. Here they may revel in security. No island breaks its surface; nor is there a single rock or bank which would afford the least shelter to the fowler. Pressing on, I came to a stone bridge which spans a narrow inlet communicating with the sea. Two fine ducks sped through the air above me, which, on examining through the glass, I perceived were a pair of the golden-eye (*Anas clangula*).

Crossing the bridge, and turning along another shore, the nature of the ground became more marshy; then, gently rising, somewhat gravelly and bare, and scantily relieved with irregular patches of stunted heather. I have been informed that a few pairs of the greater black-backed gull breed here, but the only ones I saw were the common and the herring gull. A few also of the common tern, or sea-swallow, frequented its banks. I now heard the sweet, soft, whistling cry of the ringed plover (*Charadrius hiaticula*), and, looking round, I quickly perceived one of these very elegant little birds flying by; while others were running over the grassy hillocks and along the most uneven ridges. Like their larger congener, the peewit, they chiefly give utterance to their note when on the wing, running, immediately they alight, at a great pace along the ground, and suddenly rising again with vast ease and quickness. I shot one on this spot, and in the course of my walk two others. I expected to find plenty of the common sandpiper (*Totanus hypoleucos*), as I believe they frequent this place at times in great numbers; but on this occasion I did not see one. After a brisk walk of about three-quarters of a mile, I sprang a few dunlin (*Tringa variabilis*), who usually flew rapidly across an arm of the loch, and generally lit upon some muddy flat projecting into very shallow water. I followed up some of these birds, and on firing winged two of them at a shot; rushing into the water, I secured them both in very nice condition and good plumage. I afterwards killed two more—one, in particular being a fine adult bird. This I have of course added to my collection.

I now reached some very curious perpendicular stones, standing up at various distances apart, upon the bare turf, in a striking manner, and visible from a great distance. They are something similar to those at Stonehenge, with the exception that they have no top or cross stone from one to another. The most celebrated of them all, I am sorry to say, is not now standing. It was used from time out of mind as a "plighting-stone," being perforated with a curious hole through which lovers were accustomed to exchange their vows and pledges of attachment. They were doubtless the places of worship of the ancient Scandinavians.

"And there in many a stormy vale
The Scald had told his wondrous tale,
And many a Runic column high
Had witnessed grim idolatry."
Lay of Last Minstrel.

I felt that I was treading ground eminently classic —the objects before me having been visited and alluded to by the elegant author of the 'Pirate.' At this point, a low solid piece of rough masonry, half bridge and half embankment, separates the two lochs. Crossing this, and continuing for a short distance along the second and somewhat larger sheet of water, a few ducks rose from their feeding-ground far away along the distant shore, and made straight across to where I was standing. No possible object of the smallest dimensions offered the slightest means of covert or concealment; so my only chance consisted in remaining perfectly steady and motionless. They were evidently making for the open sea, and so, flying straight up wind, passed in a direct line far above my head. I fired on the instant, and evidently struck my bird—a fine drake; but not being loaded with green cartridge, my only chance, I did no further execution.

Leaving this spot I proceeded along the edge of the original loch. I now discovered I had no more powder; but having bagged as many birds as I could conveniently prepare the skins of at one time, I had no reason to regret the absence of a further supply.

Nothing is so deceiving as water. I had set myself to make a complete circuit of this loch, and I had enough to do, by dint of hard walking, to effect my object and return to Stromness before dark. I had a great deal of hard and rough ground to pass over before I could regain any sort of road; and a long shallow bay running some distance up a marshy valley, involved a much larger circuit than I had included in my geographical calculation.

Far, very far, out of gunshot from the shore, upon a small insulated rock, I could discern a minute black object. Straining intently through my glass, I was delighted to observe a hen merganser (*Mergus serrator*) resting perfectly motionless, except when she now and then lowered her pointed head to plume and smooth her breast-feathers. Still more delighted was I to see, diving and sporting in the adjacent water, no less than twenty-one young ones.

Wonderful is the instinct and beautiful the provision which teaches these wild and wary birds to choose and take advantage of, for the purposes of incubation, spots the most inaccessible and difficult of approach. It would have tried the cunningest devices of the most experienced stalker to carry her well-fortified position; and, conscious of her full security, she proudly rested upon this single stone; and had I been armed with the most scientific weapon of offence, I could not have found it in my heart to have carried devastation into her domestic circle. I remained for a long time watching the scene with a perfect trance of pleasure, and then continued on my way. I have since obtained a pair of these birds from this loch in excellent plumage.

Nothing further worthy of remark took place during the remainder of my most pleasing walk, as, after a lengthened tramp, I halted my weary steps upon the threshold of my lodging, and the aroma of a welcome dinner descended even to the door.

CHAPTER IV.

"Jam varias pelagi volucres et quæ Asia circum
Dulcibus in stagnis rimantur prata Caystri,
Certatim largos humeris infundere rores,
Nunc caput objectare fretis, nunc currere in undas,
Et studio incassum videas gestire lavandi."
VIRG. *Georg.* Lib. 1. 383.

THE weather on the following day was stormy and boisterous to a degree. Heavy showers of rain succeeded each other with obstinate determination. The white breakers in the open sea were fierce and frolicsome, and nothing was to be done in the open air without the natural accompaniment of a very complete drenching.

It is in such weather as this that the sportsman will look after his guns. It is not the influence of the sea air alone that does the harm, but the combined effects of sea air and rain, I especially notice, cause the greatest amount of oxidation. Rainy days, however, when not of too long continuance, are by no means unwelcome to the bird collector, as on these occasions he is able to bestow unremitting attention to the due preparation of his specimens.

I was kept a close prisoner on the present occasion; and the day succeeding, though treacherously wayward in its uncertain symptoms of fair and foul, at last took a turn unmistakeably threatening, and then fairly burst into a gale—impetuous, gloomy and wet.

On the morning of the 8th of June this provoking conflict of the elements assumed a calmer and more peaceful aspect; and having been now for so long a period solely dependant upon land excursions by reason of the continued inclemency of the weather, and as the morning sun beamed brightly, and the wind blew steadily from the south-east with a brisk breeze, and the sea, though running somewhat strong, showed evident tokens of a more tractable disposition, I was mainly desirous of making the circuit of some of the smaller southern islands, or trying my good fortune in my favourite pursuit in the vicinity of the far-famed cliffs of Hoy.

Mr. Joseph Dunn, the animal preserver of this town, possesses a very cleverly built and rapid-sailing little craft, now riding at her anchor in the bay. Having repaired to his house, and discussed the feasibility of my intentions, he was at first somewhat dissuasive; and on account of the tide being now upon the flow, and the consequent late hour at which the ebb would commence, it was possible we might not be able to effect our return before the hour of ten at night. He was evidently testing the firmness of my resolution, so

I at once expressed my firm determination to start immediately, and adding that I was prepared to risk whatever consequences might ensue.

Preparations being rapidly effected for a start, our sails were set; the canvass strained upon the breeze, and the gallant little vessel, buoyant as a cork, sped along the rippling sea, apparently as intent as her occupants upon the full enjoyment of exciting sport. While rounding a point of a small island, on which, as marking the entrance to the bay, rests upon its solid freestone foundations the " lower lighthouse," looking, with its short truncated tower and lantern surmounted with its leaden dome, like a building that embraces both the style and proportions of an astronomical observatory and a Turkish mosque, the wind slightly shifted to the S.S.E., the sea began perceptibly to drop, the angry little breakers in the open water rose in their strength but sank in weakness, the effervescence of their subsiding fury being more agreeably succeeded by that continuous bubbling echo which marks the speed with which her cutwater divides every opposing riplet, speeding swiftly onwards in her merriment. We had to tack pretty sharply, as the breeze rose more briskly along the lee shore of the island. When getting upon the second or third tack, and gaining the more open water at every stride, Hoy Head, our point of rendezvous, standing out in all its indistinct and naked ruggedness, loomed upon the starboard bow.

On these occasions my skipper Dunn takes the helm; and in this squally and dangerous channel I gladly leave to his experienced hand the entire disposition and working of the boat. Seated well forward, I rest at my ease; my gun loaded with cartridge and shot, as the case may be, and ready to take instant advantage of any opportunity that the sea or the rocks may offer. Surely the language of the poet Gray must have been intended as a vaticination of this occasion:

> "Fair laughs the morn, and soft the zephyr blows,
>   While proudly riding o'er the azure realm,
>   In gallant trim the gilded vessel goes;
>   Youth at the prow, and Pleasure at the helm."

It is but seldom that the wind sets in this quarter, which is the only one available for approaching these rocks sufficiently close to effect any desirable execution. Scanning the surface of the open water, and somewhat to leeward of our course, a small black speck is occasionally visible.

With a word to Joseph, the helm slightly turns, and we bear down upon it at a steady pace. I now raise my gun and kill a black guillemot (*Uria grylle*), but it was too much shot in the head to be of any use to me. It is a pretty sight to see these birds floating on the moving mass of water, rising and falling, diving and reappearing again with great expertness. They are to my thinking a remarkably beautiful bird, most especially in their present summer plumage. The even, solid rich black of the entire back and breast feathers, only relieved by the marked white patch upon the wings; the brilliant vermilion legs and feet; the exquisite brown of the irides, are all heightened by its rather dumpy but compact and very neat form. This bird changes its plumage in a much more prominent manner than most of its class, in each season of the year; and I have been fortunate in obtaining specimens of each stage.

By-and-bye, a solitary shag (*Carbo cristatus*), here provincially termed the scarfe, rests upon the wave like an impersonation of mortality; but rises lazily upon the wing, as we draw upon his track. I am very desirous to add one of these gentlemen to my collection, and so shall strain every nerve to-day. They seem completely at home, when out upon their fishing forays, both above and below the surface of the watery element, swimming with great ease and at a rapid pace, and diving with well-known agility and power. When swimming they seem to be continually in the act of sipping and drinking the water, tossing up their long ugly heads ceaselessly to swallow the same. Sundry others appear, and, as we approach, offer seemingly a fair shot, but dive or fly uninjured by the charge. There are days and states of the wind and sea when these birds will allow the boat to approach them wonderfully close, but on most occasions they are wary and shy to a degree. On the present occasion Joseph gave me very little hope of obtaining a specimen unless any very lucky chance should turn up. With the exception of the few cases I have mentioned, both the sea and the air were literally barren of any living thing; and it would have been difficult to have persuaded oneself that the lapse of a few short moments would witness the very opposite extreme, almost amounting to redundance.

Measuring to the utmost the fast-dying currents of the breeze, we now draw near the magnificent extremity of Hoy Island, formed at this point by varied rocky coves of gently-rising craig, and beautifully backed by the cone-shaped hill of Hoy, towering to the right in the memorable and stupendous Head. Raising my glass, as we approached, and carefully scrutinising every nook and cranny, my delight was unbounded at the aspect of the scene; but when the eye was enabled to take in a wider grasp by a nearer approach, words must fail in making description simulate even a faint reality of that which met its gaze. Resting upon every possible projection, and upon innumerable ledges, so small, narrow, and constrained, that to all appearance there was scarcely space for a mouse's thoroughfare, that lovely bird the kittiwake (*Larus tridactylus*) abounded in myriads and myriads; and, while our closer neighbourhood was the signal for thousands to circle far aloft and fill the air "with sounds discordant in sonorous chaos," others rested in vacant immobility, looking like stuffed specimens effectively arranged upon a noble mass of artificial rockwork for some Brobdignagian museum. Nothing can exceed the unsullied cleanliness of these birds. In no single instance can you observe a feather draggled, or soiled, or ruffled; the snowy whiteness of their plump, smooth breasts, surpassing in clearness the chastest lustre of the spring-born lily, or the unspotted surface of the winter's drift. Far above, upon the lofty grassy steeps, but more sparingly disposed, the herring gull as usual may be seen to pair. A few razorbills have taken up their quarters in the lower crannies, and, resting upright on their short, flat feet, scrutinise our movements with a grave attention, like the bench of bishops watching with absorbed gaze the progress of a warm debate.

So beautiful, so very beautiful, was the sight that I paused long and longer still ere I dared to fire my gun, and thus introduce discord and confusion into this magnificently grouped array. I was also undesirous to do so before I had further inspected the scene while under its present aspect of comparative repose. Accordingly, striking sail and depending on the oars, we now rounded a bluff rocky headland, and entered a more cavernous and indented inlet overhung by a frowning and tremendous height. Here a variation in detail occurred, and the scene appeared to shift and alter like the changes in a play; illustrating in a beautiful manner the interesting fact that each species of bird, even in this limited space, frequents, during the all-important incubatory process, its own special locality chosen by itself, according to its nature and position, perfectly distinct from the rest—bounded by a land-mark as rigidly observed as those of neighbours in a well-regulated kingdom, and wisely and accurately adapted to the nature and habits of the bird. Do you remember Luciana's words in the "Comedy of Errors?"

> "There's nothing, situate under heaven's eye,
> But hath his bound, in earth, in sea, in sky :
> The beasts, the fishes, and the winged fowls,
> Are their males' subject, and at their controuls:
> Men, more divine, the masters of all these,
> Lords of the wide world, and wild watery seas,
> Indued with intellectual sense and souls,
> Of more pre-eminence than fish and fowls,
> Are masters to their females and their lords :
> Then let your will attend on their accords."

Far above, out of harm's reach, the dark and gloaming shags were resting on their nests, constructed on projections apparently not half big enough to hold them, and looking no bigger than rooks. Oh! how easy to shoot them as they sit, and thus bag any number to your heart's content. But no. Distance, which lends enchantment to most views, only causes here a deceptive mortification. I fire occasional shots, but their only effect is to cause the birds aimed at to drop off their retreat, and fly and dive away, apparently rejoicing in a charmed existence. Joseph, now sarcastically smiling, suggests the advisability of rounding the next point and commencing more successful operations against the guillemot. But I am rampant as to ultimate success, and determined that I will not raise the siege till some of the inhabitants succumb.

Scrutinising with the utmost minuteness every object in the field of view, I can just observe, peering from the dark recesses of a craggy gorge, which, if it had been somewhat larger and deeper, might be aptly termed a cave, two of these birds, within comparatively easy range, seated on a flat, broad ledge, the female resting on her nest, and the male bird close beside her in patriarchal and sedate solemnity. The steep scarped sides of the chasm sloping abruptly into deep, calm water, formed a spot of fearful association amid the echoing turmoil and angry lashings of a tumultuous sea.

Bringing in the boat as near as was attainable, I raised my gun and fired at the male bird as he was on the point of leaving the rock. It is remarkable what a blow these thick-skinned, close-feathered sea-birds must receive to effect any fatal execution. Having received the charge, he flew forward off the rock and downwards to the water, resorting to their usual and often too-successful plan of diving amongst the submerged seaweed. On first rising to the surface, however, he showed certain symptons of being most hard hit, though of not giving up the contest without, what turned out, an extremely exciting struggle. Still able to exert his wonderful powers of diving, but too weak to use his wings either in the way of progression or descent, he led us a chase of no short duration. While I worked the oars, Joseph, boat-hook in hand, stood at the head of the boat, ready to strike whenever he appeared within reach at the surface of the water. After a few ineffectual struggles, he reappeared, dived, and dived again, more and more exhausted, but was at last dispatched, and safely secured and placed on board. He turned out to be a very first-rate specimen of his class, nicely and cleanly shot, and having a very fine topknot or crest — which I had good reason to expect would be found wanting (as these birds were now fast casting the same) — fully and maturely developed.

We now rowed back to the spot, and found the female still sitting on the nest, but wavering whether to stay or to depart. I fired, and she too performed a similar manœuvre, flying down to the water, which involved another chase; but being more severely wounded, she succumbed within a shorter period.

My ambition was now rather fired than satisfied, and I determined to attempt to take the nest. Joseph was loud in prohibitory interjection, and was for rowing hastily away, and quenching my aspirations in a change of scene. "You must not attempt such a thing," said he: "the rocks are as slippery as they are deceptive." Ordering him to approach the rock as near as circumstances allowed, and perceiving that the water was sufficiently deep to prevent any serious consequences if I chanced to fall, I leapt from the boat, and clung for a moment to a point of rock to regain my balance, as the words "Whatever you do, take care, sir!" echoed in my ears. I was chiefly apprehensive on account of the iron nails in my boots being most unadapted for a rocky surface, and from which I had received a painful lesson on a previous occasion. Taking every and cautious advantages of the various sinuosities and inequalities of craig, and expecting every moment to find myself taking an involuntary "header," I slowly gained or rather crawled up to the very ledge on which the nest was built. This turned out to be wider, and consequently safer, than it had appeared from the water below. Along it I proceeded slowly and cautiously on my hands and knees, when my progress was stopped by a large notch or intervening space; looking down which, I perceived the dark green water below seething in the echoing cavern in a manner which caused a disagreeable sort of sickening giddiness. Controlling this, however, and balancing myself as well as I was able, I could just reach the nest upon the opposite side, in which I found three eggs. At this point, moreover, so offensive was the stench of putrefying sea-weed and dead fish that it almost caused me to recoil from the undertaking. Depositing the eggs, one in my pocket and the other two in my hand, I slowly but more confidently retraced my steps, and having delivered them safely into Joseph's hand, returned in the same manner for the nest. This, which is rudely but ingeniously constructed of the large dead stalks and roots of seaweed, the centre being lined with dead coarse grass, formed an extensive but very grewsome handful. Having brought this also in safety down to a level with the boat, it was received by Joseph on the rudder, as, having hitherto hardly dared to speak, I now restepped on board, and joyfully participated in the smile of triumph which welcomed my return.

" Not so bad for a beginning," I observed, as Joseph added that this was the first instance of birds, nest, and eggs, having been secured in one day. I shot one other bird, which fell perfectly dead, as an extra specimen; and then, having reloaded, we rowed gently on and round the next turn of the cliff. Here the scene again slightly altered, and only tended by its varying novelty to enhance it as a spectacle of surpassing ornithological interest. This face of the rock was positively peopled by birds of many kinds, but still the same rule of locality and distinctive position of each kind was adhered to in a marked degree.

Upon a limited slightly-slanting ledge, within easy range, a company of the common guillemot (*Uria troile*) were "standing easy;" some apparently engaged in close conversation, and others motionless and in the drollest attitudes. Many individuals were flying and reflying from and to the spot, and a similar scene, accompanied by the mingled hum of busy and contented clamour, was going on in every crevice from the water to the summit of the cliff. In other spots the razorbills were seen to thickly congregate in animated groups; while, far above, the little rock-pipit and the common starling I observed building in close contiguity with those of the more rapacious birds who have placed their nests secure from any molestation, save that of the craigsman on his giddy rope; while upon the utmost peak the kingly eagle forms his cradled eyrie in impregnable security.

These noble birds are getting extremely scarce of late years, though they are carefully preserved by the proprietor, J. Heddle, Esq., and a pair which have been known to settle here year after year have only been very casually noticed in the course of the present season, and have not as yet taken up their permanent abode. In the old chronicles of the island I find these words: "There are many eagles, especially at the west end of the main, and in Choye. I was very well informed that an eagle did take up a swaddled child a month old, which the mother had laid down until she went to the back of the peat stack at Honton Head, and carried it to Choye, *viz.* four miles, which being discovered by a traveller, who heard the lamentations of the mother, four men went presently thither in a boat, and, knowing the eagle's nest, found the child, without any prejudice done to it."

Reverting to the proximity of nests, I observe an announcement in the 'Court Journal' of this week of curious ornithological interest; "On the Ryes Hall farm near Sudbury, Suffolk, there is a nest containing six young hawks, an owl's nest with five young ones, a starling's nest with six young ones, and another with three young ones, all on the same tree, and within about two feet of each other."

This vast assemblage of the feathered tribe gave one a good idea of the uproar that ensues after the explosion of a cannon from a passing steamer, and I quote the following from Miss Sinclair's 'Shetland.' "Our steamboat passed near Coppensha, one of the Orkneys, which presents a gigantic barricade of rocks, inhabited by millions of birds, which we saw, though I had not the time to count them, sitting in rows like charity children, with black heads and white tippets, ranged along every crevice in the cliffs. Captain Phillips caused several guns to be fired, when an uproarious noise ensued, which can be compared to nothing but the hurraing of a whole army. It seemed like a long loud roar, accompanied by the echoing and re-echoing of guns—a whole platoon of cannon, till at length I fancied that the commotion could scarcely have been more deafening from the mob and artillery of London on the day of her Majesty's coronation. Above, below, and around, the sea, air, and rocks seemed all one living mass of birds, screaming at the full pitch of their voices, rushing through the air, careering to the very clouds, flickering in circles over head, zigzagging all around us, and then dropping like a shower into the ocean. Nothing in the way of animal life ever amazed me so much. I wonder if any one on earth can imagine it?—no, certainly not! seeing is believing, and nothing else will help you."

When the quantity of fish that each of these birds can consume at a single meal is taken into consideration, and the number of young ones that they will have to provide for in a few weeks, it remains a matter of marvel that sufficient food should be concentrated in these parts to supply the wants of such a multitude;

F

and yet "not one sparrow falleth to the ground without your Father's knowledge."

In single and rare instances the bridled or ringed guillemot (*Uria lacrymans*) has been known to breed here. It is distinguished by a slight white streak running backwards and downwards in a curved line from the eye. As the common guillemot could of course be easily enough shot, Joseph and I concentrated all our endeavours to descry, if possible, any of these birds. At last to my joy, Joseph pointed out a single pair, in the centre of the group of guillemots I first noticed on the lower ledge. Rowing up, I waited till I observed them so close together that it seemed easy enough to kill them at a shot. I fired; but instead of dropping, both birds flew away apparently unscathed. This was a very grievous disappointment; but such is the fortune of war.

It is remarkable what a power of flight these birds possess, considering the smallness of the wing. The muscles of the joint, however, are very strong and tough, and the vibration extremely rapid and sustained.

After waiting and watching the return and departure of separate birds for a very long time without avail, one of my friends revisited the ledge, when I fired and brought him to the water, where he gave us a long and anxious chase. In the midst of it, however, to Joseph's consternation, I fired just above his head, and dropped the other bird quite dead as he sped along in full career above me. They were both first-rate specimens;, and their capture may be looked upon as a piece of real good fortune, as they turned out to be the only pair I saw during my sojourn in the Orkneys. I now killed a pair of the common guillemot (*Uria troile*), and we then proceeded to get the sail up for our voyage home.

The whole of this time we had been dancing about on a nasty sort of heaving swell, and I began to feel a very disagreeable qualmishness. This, when about half-way home, reached its climax, and then, and not till then, was I able to enjoy luncheon. As we got out in the open water, I shot a male and female puffin (*Mormon fratercula*). Stretching well away with the tide, what little breeze there was now gradually dropped, and our return voyage was therefore very protracted, but not without incident. We passed three bottle-nosed whales ploughing along, rising, falling, and playing in their native element—extruding at times their black dorsal fins high into the air. The afternoon, fast passing into evening serene and beautiful, settled into an almost dead calm. The sail flapped — almost hung — in lazy uncertainty, and, though our tacks were long and frequent, we were really but dependant upon tide. We reached Stromness at a quarter to nine, p.m., and I was not sorry for a hearty meal.

The night closed in (if nights they can be called in this undarkened region) with the full glory of a crimson sunset, and all surrounding nature, properly imbued with the spirit of charity, shared with willing emphasis the general repose.

CHAPTER V.

"After long storms and tempests overblowne,
 The sunne at length his joyous face doth cleare;
So when as Fortune all her spight hath showne,
 Some blissful hours at last must needs appeare;
Else should afflicted wights oftimes despeire."

SPENSER.

SUCH a day as yesterday was not to be forgotten, even in the matter of weather alone, and the more so because the four succeeding ones have been especially distinguished for the opposite extreme; storm, rain, and cold prevailing to such an unwonted degree as to cause even the inhabitants of these islands to exclaim. There is an advertisement in one of the papers this week (I need not say which) from a celebrated luminary, which is so neatly worded and pointed that I cannot pass it over:

"Clerk of the Weather Office.
"Notice is hereby given, that in consequence of the zodiac being taken up for repairs, there will be no summer or autumn this year. All contracts made on the understanding that the seasons would go on as usual, hiring of country houses and of moors, arrangements for tours, promises to marry, and the like, are

null and void. The winter quarter begins on the 1st July, proximo, and terminates some time next year.

"(Signed)   PHŒBUS APOLLO."

The weather has been extremely unsettled, unpleasant, and rough, in the early part of the present morning; nevertheless I have set off with my knapsack and gun, intending to take a line across the island "as the crow flies" (which I have specially observed in the north is most wonderfully straight), in the direction of Bin' Scarth, and take the chance of finding Mr. S———h, the Banker, and Russian, Prussian, French, American, and Swedish Consul in Orkney, at home. I carry a letter of introduction to him from Dr. S———r, of Wick.

I retraced the original country as far as the noble Loch of Steanhouse. Then, striking off across a considerable hill, I mounted its heathery side and revelled in the freedom of a cooler breeze. Having made about two-thirds of its ascent, surprising on its unfrequented braes the timid and solitary harè, as, bounding away aslant the slope, she rested upon some higher ledge, sharply upraising her elegant ears, and carefully reconnoitring with her soft and prominent eyes the scene of her unceremonious flight, I hear a sweet flute-like cry with which I happen to be unacquainted. List! I hear it again!—" tweet," " tweet," " tweet"—

among the heather. It is that very pretty bird the golden plover (*Charadrius pluvialis*), which, somewhat wilder than the rest of its species, runs along the sandy knoll, then flies a space, and alighting, soon renews its plaintive note, musically alternating with its mate's reply. These birds were in this instance too wild to shoot, so, rounding and descending a neighbouring brow, I rested for awhile to observe the flight of one of the larger hawks about the summit of the hill. I now inquired my way at a little ragstone mountain-hut, and then, pressing down the slope, made across a somewhat extensive tract of flat bog-land that formed the intervening space between this and another range of low rocky hills beyond.

About the centre of this peaty but partly-cultivated vale I crossed a little burn whose waters bubbled onwards to the loch, and here I had the pleasure of obtaining in very perfect plumage a pair of that very-delicately-pencilled bird the redshank (*Totanus calidris*). The male bird arose very suddenly some distance before I approached the stream, and, having received my charge of small-shot, flew in widening circles, apparently untouched, higher and further up the valley, and then fell, burying its crimson beak in the soft soil. It would have ill become me, after thus ruthlessly desecrating their domestic hearth, to have left his now sonorous mate to endure the cares and sorrows of disconsolate widowhood; so, after indulging a lengthened observation of her beautiful airy unlaboured mode of flight, I raised my second barrel and consigned her to a timely and inglorious decease. I have no doubt but that they possessed a nest somewhere thereabouts, but though I searched diligently I was unsuccessful in discovering it. I have not yet had an opportunity of studying closely the habits of this fairy of the air, as the present pair are the first of the kind that I have seen, though I hear that round the smaller lochs of this district they are sometimes to be met with in considerable numbers.

I scarcely ever take a walk in this island but I see the little wheatéar (*Sylvia œnanthe*), in its mottled plumage, jerking forth its short harsh note, darting from hillock to hillock, or perching upon the pointed rocks that shelve upon the shore.

Crossing a thickly-covered space of stunted broom and crisp elastic peat-moss, intersected with deep channels of black water, I sprung a single snipe, but was unprepared for his sudden appearance. Mounting and descending the opposite hill, a very prettily situated modern residence, surrounded with substantial evidences of gentlemanly comfort and more advanced cultivation, and flanked by a neatly-kept homestead of no small extent and farm accomodation, formed the more prominent feature of a very striking and picturesque landscape. Making my way up its steep and gravelly approach, I discovered I had not been wrong in concluding this to be the object of my lengthened ramble. Mr. S——h I had the pleasure of finding at home, and I gladly pay a willing tribute to his generous hospitality. I stayed with him until the morning of Monday, and the freshening influences of a private bath-room, added to the various and nameless comforts which a country residence can alone supply, were doubly welcome after the toil and uncertainties of travel. In the course of conversation upon the subject of Canada, my host had reason to refer to his journal, an anecdote from which, though quite irrelevant to my present subject, I requested to be allowed to transcribe; and, craving forbearance for this digression, present it to my readers for what it is worth:

"Walking through Watertown, I had the good luck to meet a Canadian judge of my acquaintance, who gave me many curious anecdotes of Watertown and its vicinity in the war of 1812. One of these, having reference to a Mr. Spraggs, a fine-looking old man whom he pointed out as the possessor of considerable property in the town, is remarkable as being somewhat illustrative of the go-ahead character of the Americans, and of the facility with which they cleverly turn to advantage the apparently most adverse circumstances.

"Spraggs and a Mr. Fairbanks had become bound as sureties to the States Government for the safe conveyance of money from Washington for the payment of troops about to be disbanded in the neighbourhood of Watertown, at the close of the war. They had in their employment one Spiggleman, and entrusted him with a large sum in paper-money, which was packed at Washington and delivered to him for conveyance to Watertown. Spiggleman pretended that he had been robbed, and showed the hole cut in his saddle-bags, through which the parcel had been abstracted. Not crediting his story, although he exhibited a very considerable contusion on his head in corroboration, Spraggs watched nightly at his residence, while Fairbanks set off to Washington, and obtained from the treasury a fac-simile of the parcel of bills entrusted to Spiggleman. The hole cut in the saddle-bags was found too small to have admitted the abstraction of the parcel. The sureties, resolved to have back the money, urged upon Spiggleman to give them, on some pretence, a meeting at a retired place where there was a marsh and a mud-pool full of water. Here the two determined men laid hold of the miserable Spiggleman, and told him their suspicions, viz., 'That unless the money was restored they were both utterly ruined; that they had made up their minds to have the money or his life. They might just as well be hung for his death as incur the utter ruin and destitution of themselves and families. In short they were desperate.' He vehemently protested his innocence; but they seized him, and plunged him into the mud-hole, holding him betwixt them, and occasionally dipping him over head. He, however, proved obstinate, and protested his innocence until he became speechless. They pulled him out, and, rolling him on the ground he recovered, and, falling on his knees, begged hard for his life, protesting his innocence until he became speechless. Fairbanks told him that he had only spared him on the remonstrance of Spraggs; but that if he was put in a second time, he declared he should alone come out a corpse, unless he made confession. Again they plunged him in, and when just upon the point of suffocating, he shouted out, 'I will confess!' Holding his head above the water, he informed them 'that the bills were all quilted into his wife's petticoat, ready for a start to Canada; that the petticoat was at that moment lying betwixt the bed mattress in his wife's bedroom at home.'

"Fairbanks watched the culprit in that solitary spot until Spraggs went off to ascertain the truth of this story. Rushing to the house he ascertained that Mrs. Spiggleman was in the bedroom, and the door locked. Smashing it open with his foot, he found the woman in the act of putting on the petticoat, and everything apparently prepared for a start. Forcing the garment from her grasp, he rushed into the market-place of Watertown, which at that time was a mere village, waving the petticoat round his head and shouting,

'I have it!' Fairbanks, hearing the signal, dragged forward the wretched, dripping Spiggleman, and the inhabitants knocked the head out of a rum keg, and made a rejoicing.

"As Spiggleman was dragged forward, amid the hootings of the people, he was only saved from immediate and final lynch-law by a tragic event. His wife,* a very handsome young woman, rushed forward, exclaiming: 'You coward! why did you not die without confessing?' She then sprang upon the wall of the cemetery or graveyard, and, dashing over the steep banks into the river, was over the falls and drowned, before anyone could prevent her—showing that *she* at least had the determination to die rather than live under the shame of defeated rascality.

"Spraggs and Fairbanks having got possession of the cash, determined on a spec. to cover expenses before delivering it to Government. They attended a ready-money sale of war-stores, and purchased the whole, immediately retailing by another, and thus made a profit which laid the foundation, with Spraggs at least, of the largest fortune in the now large and populous city of Watertown"

The word "scarth" is Norse for *strath* or *glen*, of which this is a fair and bold example; and the house commands from the east side a most charming view of Grumbuster Holm and the island of Damsa.

A few miles to the south-east is the town of

Kirkwall, the capital of the island, and celebrated for its ancient and interesting Cathedral, dedicated to St. Magnus, and begun seven centuries ago by Ronald, Earl of Orkney. On Sunday I attended divine service at the kirk of Stenhouse on the banks of the loch, and this leads me to mention that the loch takes its name from an old stone residence no longer existing, and formerly belonging to the Balfour family.

It was a glorious, bright, breezy morning as I took leave of Bin' Scarth, and resumed my solitary ramble over the uplands. I killed in my course a golden plover (*Charadrius pluvialis*), the only one at which I had a chance, though I saw plenty. Wary as I found this bird—at this season scattered in pairs upon the hills — they, when the cold weather sets in, flock together in vast crowds. St. John, in his " Field Notes for November," says : " Late in the evening the golden plovers come in considerable numbers to the bare grass fields to feed during the night; but when the ground is hardened by frost they resort to the sands at the ebb-tide, both by night and day, Whilst the tide is high these birds fly up to the hills, resting on those places where the heather is short, and their instinct teaches them exactly when to leave the hills for the sands, as soon has the sea has receded sufficiently; and yet their principal resting-place is fully five miles inland." This particular phase of instinct is very striking, and is instanced in a still more remarkable manner in the case of the female shieldrakes when sitting on their eggs: "Although several feet underground, they know to a moment when the tide has sufficiently ebbed, and then, and only then, do they leave their nests to snatch a hasty meal on the cockles, &c., which they find on the sands." The appearance of the loch this morning was very beautiful, and often did I pause in silent contemplation. Its bright blue waters, illumined by the inconstant sun, and its white wave crests lashed into mimic fury by the uncertain wind, chased each other in ever-glistening change.

There is first-rate trout fishing in this loch. In fact, I am told that it is the finest loch trout-fishing in North Britain. The charr is also found here, and I regret exceedingly that—my occupations having been so engrossing—I have been unable to spare time to throw a fly upon its surface. After a health-giving walk I reached Stromness betimes, and, among other circumstances of the day, I met and obtained a very fine skin of the female honey buzzard (*Falco apivorus*) shot rather earlier in the season. I have a male bird already in my collection, having been trapped in the woods of Wyndyard Park, in the county of Durham.

The weather on the following day turned out most unpropitious. Were it not for this I had intended taking a sloop to the island of Sanda, a low flat sandy islet standing away to the N.E., about seven miles long by about half a mile broad.

My attractions thither lay in the fact of that elegant little bird the red-necked phalarope (*Phalaropus hyperboreus*) having been known to breed there for many years upon a small reedy loch to the north of the island. This bird is now becoming extremely rare in Britain, and but for the fact of its breeding haunts being somewhat preserved by the proprietor of the island, would soon become entirely extinct. The common shieldrake (*Anas tadorna*) also breeds here in great numbers, taking up its quarters in the rabbit-holes, from which it ignominiously expels the rightful owners.

CHAPTER VI.

" The wanderers of heaven
Each to his home retire, save those that love
To take their pastime in the troubled air,
Or skimming flutter round the dimply pool."

THOMSON.

HAVING heard that a considerable mass of reeds grew at one end of this loch, I concluded that the bald coot (*Fulica atra*) would be certainly found there ; a bird common enough on many of our southern meres, but not as yet existing in my own collection. My hypothesis turned out to be correct.

After I had surmounted the last hill that overhangs the lake, the view became very pleasant. I know not how it is, but I suppose partly from association and partly from its effect, that the sudden appearance of water in a landscape is always gladdening to my sight. I had, during the latter portion of my walk, felt considerably exhausted, owing to having imprudently carried nothing with me in the shape of luncheon ; so, resting at a cottage door, I craved, not unreluctantly, a little simple refreshment. The gude woman's interrogatories both startled and amused me. " Where do you come from?" " Are you in a consumption?"

To the first, "From London," I replied, while to the second, I observed that her delicious milk and oatcake were fast becoming amenable to a very galloping stage of that ravaging disease.

On descending to the water-side, I killed a fine specimen of the common tern (*Sterna hirundo*), after watching for some time the very beautiful and at the same time wonderful mode in which these birds obtain their food. Skimming along the water's edge, but maintaining a considerable height from its surface, they suddenly abate their speed, and hover for a moment, somewhat akin to the steady pose of the kestrel, in a very dexterous and pretty manner; they then drop down to the water almost as quickly as they rise from it, submerging nothing but the points of their beautiful vermilion mandibles, with which they seldom fail to secure their prey, usually in the shape of the tiny little sand-eel, one of the fastest inhabitants of the waters, and which they almost immediately swallow.

On the opposite side of the loch I also killed the Arctic tern (*Sterna arctica*), which swallow-like, graceful bird only differs from the common species in the upper and under mandible being one quarter of an inch shorter, and of a bright coral-red throughout its entire length. The tarsus also is shorter and the under surface of a deeper grey. In the centre of this loch is a small circular island of artificial construction, formed by the father of the present proprietor, Mr. Watt, of the House of Skael, an unpretending but rather picturesque edifice, situated on a narrow neck of land between this and the sea, and whose hospitality I shortly afterwards had the pleasure of receiving. This little island was densely covered with pairs of the black-headed gull (*Larus ridibundus*), to my taste the most elegant and beautiful of their tribe; indeed, so closely were the birds disposed, that it would seem as if the constant rising and settling of some must break the eggs of the others. They were very shy and wary, and the island being far out of gunshot, and there being no boat upon the loch, I was quite unable on this occasion to procure a single specimen. Bishop Stanley, in his remarks on this bird, mentions their breeding on a similar island in a mere about thirty miles from the sea, at Woodrising, in Norfolk.

On a subsequent occasion, while being entertained at the House of Skael—it being impossible to use a boat by reason of the shallowness of the loch, and equally impossible to wade a sufficient distance on account of the softness and depth of the sand, I succeeded in out-manœuvring and killing a pair in the following manner. Stationing myself upon a low flat of dry sand, at one end of the loch, on which I had observed these birds occasionally feeding, I remained perfectly immovable in a standing position for at least three hours; and a cutting easterly wind prevailing, I was not a little stiff at the end of that period. In the meantime, however, several of them, unable any longer to conceal their curiosity, after much uncertain evolution, and evidently bent upon reconnoitring my position, approached within fair range, maintaining a continuous and unceasing chatter. I fired several shots and killed three birds, two of which were most neatly shot, and as fine a pair as I could wish to possess. A beautiful pale roseate tint pervaded the breast feathers of the male bird.

Every now and then the whole family would rise almost to a bird, circle in mazy and noisy confusion, descend, and gradually resume their original quiet companionship. Sweeping the loch with my glass, I could perceive a small flock of ducks, probably the common wild duck, disporting themselves upon the very centre, and evidently quite conscious of security. Threading my way along the margin, the little dunlin, springing from their moist resting-spots in pairs and small companies, commenced a flight with a shrill echoing note; and when half across the loch would, as it were, change their mind, and returning with a rapid sidelong flight, resume their silent rest upon the round, half-hidden, stones. The ringed plover were numerous on the adjacent ground as usual, and warbled coyly to each other in low whistling tones. At the further end of this piece of water I could more plainly discern masses of reeds, their heads just appearing above the edge of the water. Inside these, as I expected, I observed one pair of the bald coot, floating (so lightly do these birds swim) with their buoyant bodies fully two-thirds above the surface of the water, and so alive to danger that long before I reached the low marshy portion of the shore, and had endeavoured to take advantage of the slender covert that the reeds afforded, they were sailing far away among the ducks, out upon the bosom of the loch. No precaution or manœuvre would avail, and after duly reconnoitring every portion of the soft ground, I quickly prepared and commenced to wade. Having divested myself of all superfluous apparel, I loaded with cartridge, and succeeded, slowly but surely, in gaining the deeper water, where the reeds suddenly ceased. The birds, however, provokingly suspicious, increased their distance in still greater proportion; and the bottom now becoming at every step more soft and treacherous, I was fain to make good my return, feeling much like a fly that has made its escape from the tenacious surface of a jar of treacle.

This bird builds a very ingeniously constructed floating nest, interwoven much after the fashion of an old hamper; and in a subsequent and similar foray among the reeds of another loch (the loch of Skerrie), I had the pleasure of finding one of them, though the eggs were not yet laid. These nests are prevented being carried away by floods, the materials of which they are composed being fastened to the rushes or osiers near them; but at the same time these fastenings are of such a nature as to allow of the nests rising with the water, so that no ordinary flood would expose them to the danger of submersion.

St. John observes that "he found one on a loch, which the bird had fastened on a floating tree that had grounded on a shallow, but which, having again got adrift, owing to a rise in the loch, had been driven by the wind until it stuck fast close to the shore where the old bird was still at work. One bird seems to remain on the nest while its mate brings it rushes, which the stationary bird disposes of by adding them to the already large structure, till it seems sufficiently high above the water, and solid enough to resist wind and weather. The whole nest is firm enough to bear a much greater weight than is ever imposed on it."

The red-necked phalarope has been known to breed on this water for several successive seasons, but I could not discover any substantial sign of its having frequented this locality in the course of the present year.

Before leaving this spot I wandered to the edge of the coast, and as I threaded its rugged boundary I gazed with exultation on the broad bright waters of the Atlantic Ocean dancing and heaving under a brilliant sun: the white breakers cresting the inconstant billows in the cerulean distance; and far beneath my feet along the base of the cliffs, dashing with a bursting spreading surge, and resounding with a booming echo in their hollow caves. Directing my steps homewards, a pleasant walk over the hills brought me within view of the very picturesque bay of Stromness; its waters quiescent, with a glassy smoothness, beautifully reflected the hulls and rigging of two noble vessels belonging to the Hudson's Bay Company, which have this day put in here for a fortnight, on their voyage to that territory. Their annual visit to these islands causes a marked stir and excitement in the town and neighbourhood, and their arrival was announced by a lengthened *feu de joie*, the echo of which was dying away among the hills as I commenced my walk this morning. It was a soothing lovely view, heightened and made rich beyond expression by the varied hues of a fading streaky sunset.

> "Hoc etiam, emenso quum jam decedet Olympo,
> Profuerit meminisse magis: nam sæpe videmus
> Ipsius in vultu varios errare colores:
> Cæruleus pluvium denuntiat."
>
> VIRG. *Georg.* Lib. 1.

CHAPTER VII.

"Rebus angustis animosus atque
Fortis appare : sapienter idem
Contrahes vento nimium secundo
Turgida vela."

HOR. Book II. Ode X.

A GLANCE at the map will exhibit a perfect cluster of small islets dotting the more sheltered water between the islands of Hoy and South Ronaldsha. There is no doubt that had I been in these parts three weeks before, I should have had ample opportunity of obtaining a more extensive variety of the genus Palmipedes. The great northern diver (*Colymbus glacialis*), the red-throated ditto (*Colymbus septentrionalis*), wigeon (*Anas Penelope*), goldeneye (*A. clangula*), eider duck (*A. mollissima*), velvet scoter (*A. fusca*), scaup (*A. marila*), longtailed duck (*A. glacialis*), Sclavonian grebe (*Podiceps cornutus*), &c. &c., had just taken their departure, and nothing but the merest chance could afford the slightest prospect of success as far as these birds are concerned.

It was a most auspicious morning, as, rising refreshed and ready for action, I found a note on my breakfast-table from Joseph Dunn, intimating that, as all things wore so favourable an aspect, the boat would be in readiness by ten o'clock.

Once more, then, we are under weigh, her head to the southward, a fair breeze prevailing, and our little craft careering madly " o'er the glad waters of the dark blue sea." As we cleared the entrance to the bay, we passed under the wake of the magnificent Hudson's Bay ships, proudly resting on their cables in the roads. After a few tacks, bay, town, ships, and all the various prominences of the fast-receding landscape, dwindled into indistinctness, and then became gradually invisible. Joseph now caught sight of a northern diver, and the concomitant excitement which ensued must have agreeably amused Mr. D——, a young gentleman staying in the island on account of his health, and whom I had invited to join us in our day's sail. These birds, at all times the most active, wary, and adroit of any that frequent our shores, are most difficult to procure, even when the presence of numbers affords a choice of shot. This one must have been quite, the laggard of the season, as it was the only one that was observed, ere it dived to be seen no more.

In about an hour we rounded the point of Holm, on which were a few common gulls, and entered the rapid and (at times) most dangerous waters of the Scapa Flow. Here and there were single instances, or pairs, as the case might be, of the greater blackbacked gull

(*Larus marinus*), gliding on graceful pinion at a great height, and never presenting themselves under any circumstances within even respectable rifle range. Oh! how I longed for one of these majestic aëronauts! There is something strikingly beautiful in the whole contour of this fine bird, especially when seen under the advantage of its fully-matured summer plumage. The rich glossy indigo of the back and wings contrasting in the most marked and bold manner with the snowy softness of its convex bosom; its full well-proportioned neck, and half-vigilant half-sleepy eye; its compressed upper mandible, giving it a sort of superciliously sarcastic expression; its ship-shape, tapering form; the bright pale flesh-colour of its legs and feet; each and all contribute to embellish, in a striking degree, a most dignified elegance of form. A full adult bird is one-third larger than the herring gull in size. The lesser blackbacked gull is a minor model of the above, but differing in the colour of the legs and feet, which are of a bright gamboge-yellow, the former becoming paler upwards, and the claws black.

Mr. Scarth has told me that whenever these birds are to be seen hovering along the shore, a close observer need never be without fish for dinner. The principal food of this gull is the flounder; which fish, when the tide recedes, has the power of immediately burying itself in the wet sand, where it remains until the return of the tide. Before, however, it is able to effect this, this bird often pounces down upon it. By hurrying to the spot, therefore, wherever this bird is seen to drop in its flight, the fish may generally be dug out and secured.

A finer, larger, rarer, and perhaps still more noble-looking bird, is the glaucous gull (*Larus glaucus*), but there must be something more than usually attractive to allure this bird within gunshot. To my great good fortune, however, a dead whale has been lately stranded upon this coast, from which Joseph has succeeded in shooting me a really magnificent specimen while in the act of feeding on the carcass. They are known to follow floating animal matter for thousands of miles; and I am very proud of the present specimen. It is termed "the burgomaster" by the Dutch, being the title of their chief magistrate; and it is a name extremely well chosen, since no other gull dares to dispute its authority whenever it chooses to exert it. A constant attendant on the whale-fishers whenever they are busied in cutting up a whale, it hovers over the carcass, and, having fixed its eye on a choice morsel of blubber or flesh, which some other of the gull tribe has secured for itself, down it comes, and forcing it to abandon the prize, carries it off as its own; or, if pressed by hunger, will sometimes even fall upon one of the smaller sea-birds, and devour it whole. Thus, one of them was shot in the Polar expedition under Sir Edward Parry, which immediately disgorged a little auk or Greenland dove (*Alca alle*), and, on opening him, another was discovered still undigested. I would wish to have enlarged upon this bird to a much greater extent, but this being the first and only specimen I have met with, I have had hitherto no opportunity of studying it as minutely as I could have wished. It gives me an indescribable sense of pleasure to observe these free happy fellows dividing the liquid air with their long expansive wings with easy gliding sweep. "No human ingenuity or skill could ever have devised so perfect an instrument as the bird's wing for its intended purpose: so light and yet so powerful; so spacious when spread out, and yet so compact, and gathered into so small a compass when not wanted. We may form some idea of the extraordinary strength of a bird, from knowing that the great muscle which chiefly regulates the movements of its wing weighs more than all the other muscles of its body put together, constituting not less than one-sixth part of the whole body; whereas those of the human body are not one-hundredth part as large in proportion."*

There is scarcely anything that, to my mind, so effectually realises a state of existence completely divested of sordid, selfish earthliness as the observing a being resting or moving in airy space, self-sustaining, self-reliant. There is something ethereal, almost

* Stanley's "Birds."

heavenly, in the spectacle. And thus it is, I have no doubt, that human imagination affixes wings to the angels, the messengers of Heaven, fleeting on their errands of wrath or glory, or beating upwards the souls of the departed. Moreover, every action of these propelling *membra*—the folding and closing of them; the fanning of, and nestling under, wings—is beautiful and soothing, both in reality and by metaphor. Even these very birds, resting upon the most tempestuous seas, and haunting these narrow and dangerous straits, have been accounted by the sailors of these northern latitudes, spirits of pernicious omen :

" The black'ning wave is edged with white;
To inch and rock the sea-mews fly :
The fishers have heard the water-sprite,
Whose screams forbode that wreck is nigh."
Lay of the Last Minstrel.

We had not long left the Holm skerrie, picking up fresh speed with every gentle gust; I was leaning lazily on the gunwale, descanting on the merits of the day, or discussing the points of difference or resemblance between the various birds that met our gaze ; when, just as we were shifting on the starboard tack, and bringing up her head to the wind, a lesser black-backed gull (*Larus fuscus*), which I had for some time been steadily watching, approached so near, in one of his long, easy, characteristic sweeps, that I gave him the contents of my cartridge-barrel at a venture. I felt from the first the shot had told, though he exhibited but slender evidence of the same, and veered away so far that I could only trace his progress with the aid of my glass. He had almost vanished in the far distance, a small and indistinct black speck, when his motions all at once manifested an absence of control, and falling briskly on the wind, down, down, down in slow and lessening circlets, descended spirally to the wave.

"*Io triumphe!*" was the cry, as we bore down with all sail, and at last found the object of our search floating placidly and dead upon the tossing wave. He proved a first-rate specimen, and a welcome addition to my collection.

Changing our course again we steered for the " Barrel of Butter," a large herring-barrel placed upon the top of a tall post, to warn the inexperienced from a dangerous pile of rocks in the very centre of the Flow. Such small isolated spots as this are often the favourite resting-places of some of the rarer birds, and I was fortunate in obtaining a beautiful pair of the little auk which had been shot at this point at an earlier period of the season. These birds are becoming extremely rare in these parts of late years. There are several persons now living who remember the great auk (*Alca impennis*) breeding on the rocks at Papa Westra, when they as children have taken their eggs and broken them in wanton sport. Sad, indeed, is it to hear such melancholy evidence, and which each succeeding year, too, incontrovertibly confirms, of the influence which thoughtless man is continuously and culpably exerting to thin the numbers of, if not to exterminate from amongst us, the charming companions which the Creator has formed for our mutual enjoyment.

The island of Cava hove now upon our right, and after cruising along its rocky shore I landed upon its southern side, Several terns were dancing in the air, and I here first made the acquaintance of Richardson's skua (*Lestris Richardsoni*), one of the tribe of parasite gulls, flying with hawk-like swiftness along the shingly slope, until it disappeared from view beyond a mass of supervening rock. They maintain an unceasing warfare with the terns, bullying the poor little birds to such an extent that they are obliged to eject the food they have obtained, which the skua immediately swallows. There were several oystercatchers on the rocks, and on the opposite side I found a greater black-backed gull feeding, but did not succeed in bagging him.

We now sailed round the island of Fara, and along the shores of Flota island. These islands consist of a shapeless mass of rock, more or less precipitous; the short close turf which crowns their summits affording subsistence, such as it is, to the few sheep generally to be found upon them. Plenty of dunlin, plover, sandpipers, &c., were running here and there amongst the stones and pebbles. It was in these narrow straits that we had expected to have come across some eider duck or grebe, but, as I have previously observed, it was getting too late in the season, and not one was to be seen. The water here was intensely smooth, shining, and transparent. Several razorbills (*Alca torda*), of which I killed three, were diving or fishing singly or in flocks.

The wind now fast dropping, we rounded the southern side of Fara, and passing Rysa Little, from which a pair of the Manx shearwater * (*Puffinus anglorum*) have come into my possession, made straight across to Houton Head.

I have had a shot at a gannet, or solan goose (*Sula bassana*), as he rode upon the wind overhead. I have never yet come sufficiently near one of these remarkable birds for the shot to penetrate their tough thick skin. They are, moreover, provided with a means of introducing air between their skin and their bodies, making them light and buoyant to the last degree. They, consequently, must receive a very hard blow to bring them down from any great height. These birds are not so common in these parts as they are along the shores of the mainland of Scotland. The

---

* On the 2nd July, 1866, I descended the cliff of Altahuile, in Rathlin Island, Co. Antrim, Ireland, by means of ropes, to a depth of between sixteen and seventeen fathoms, and took the young of this bird—a little downy fledgling—capturing the old female in the nest.

beautiful mode in which they take their prey I have described in the 'Field,' in October, 1860. Stanley explains it thus: "The power which this bird possesses of inflating its skin with air induces a buoyancy which entirely prevents its diving after fish, Nature, therefore, has provided a remedy by giving an extraordinary force and rapidity of flight, in enabling the creature to dart down upon a shoal from a great height. This velocity is so prodigious that the force with which it strikes the surface of the water is sufficient to stun a bird not prepared for such a blow, or to force the water up its nostrils. But the gannet has nothing to fear from either of these causes, the front of its head being covered with a sort of horny mask, which gives it a singularly wild appearance; and it has no nostrils— a deficiency amply remedied by the above-mentioned reservoirs of air and capacity for keeping them always filled. Some notion may be formed of the rapidity of their descent by a curious mode of taking them occasionally practised by the fishermen in the north. A board is turned adrift, on which a dead fish is fastened: on seeing it the gannet pounces down, and is frequently killed or stunned by striking the board, or is secured by its sharp-pointed beak being actually driven into the wood like a nail, and holding it fast."

The gannets found in Orkney in summer probably all breed at Suliskerry, called by the Orcadians the "Stack and Skerry," forty miles due west of Stromness and this is the only breeding station of this bird anywhere nearer than St. Kilda.

It was a long but pleasant sail home. On a single rock standing out from the shore stood a pair of herring gulls, hesitating in a very evident manner as to whether or not it was time to rise upon the wing. Wishing to uncharge my gun, I fired, and killed them both at a shot. On a small skerrie off Cubister were some scarfes, amongst which we could distinguish one eider duck, or dunter, as they are here termed. I managed to get a fair shot at it, but unfortunately missed the bird. A few of these ducks remain here to breed, but we did not succeed in finding any of their nests. They breed also in Rowsay and other islands, and according to St. John, upon some small islands off the Kyle of Tongue, on the north coast of Sutherland; and that splendid bird the king duck (*Anas spectabilis*) is occasionally though rarely seen in their companionship. Upon the whole they are a heavy bird upon the wing, and though strong and active in other respects, their flight appears to be more sluggish than that of other ducks. It was just about this point, a few weeks previous, that Joseph succeeded in bagging a fine male example of the velvet scoter (*Anas fusca*), which I have added to my other specimens.

Nothing could have been more unexceptionable than the day in question, but, notwithstanding its general serenity, a keen and freshening breeze had made a thick warm pilot-coat an acceptable addition to my comfort.

Many a guillemot and puffin enlivened the expanse of waters, as we conversed on many a gleeful topic, or chanted a wild stanza to the winds. As we approached the harbour I killed a couple of kittiwake gulls, to finish the bag; and as we entered the bay every feature of the ambient landscape was bathed in a flush of many-coloured light, radiating on the limpid water with a dazzling reflection, like a sheet of burnished gold:

> "The western wave was all a-flame,
> The day was well nigh done!
> Almost upon the western wave
> Rested the broad bright sun."
> *The Ancient Mariner.*

CHAPTER VIII.

> "Jam sibi tum curvis malè temperat unda carinis,
> Quum medio celeres revolant ex æquore mergi,
> Clamoremque ferunt ad littora: quumque marinæ
> In sicco ludunt *fulicæ;* notasque paludes
> Deserit atquæ altam supra volat ardea nubem."
>
> VIRGIL.

AMONG all the variety of birds of which these islands are more or less prolific in the course of the breeding season, I do not think that any has so completely roused my ardour to possess, or my ambition to obtain, as the weird-looking and voracious pelican of the ocean, the cormorant (*Carbo cormoranus*); and my zeal is, perhaps, the more excessive in the cause, by reason that Joseph (whose experience in regard to these matters I am strongly tempted to rely upon) holds out in the present case the faintest or no hope of success, inasmuch as their haunts are situated at a marvellous distance from any position of ordinary accessibility.*

---

* This outburst of my youthful ardour will assuredly evoke a smile from many a reader on our south and south-west coasts, where the breeding-haunts of *C. cormoranus* are so

These birds breed in great numbers upon the face of the Black Craig, but taking up their position for the purpose at such a fearful and dizzy height as completely to astonish the beholder, notwithstanding his previous experience in these matters. My only chance accordingly consisted in first gaining the foot of the craig by water, and then essaying every resource that steady shooting and length of range might liberally offer.

It will be easily understood that unless the wind were to blow steadily and lightly from the desired quarter, my efforts would not only have been fruitless, but would undoubtedly have been attended with the utmost peril. It was therefore not only indispensable that the sea should be sufficiently undisturbed to permit me to approach these rocks with impunity, but I was also desirous that it should be most especially calm and motionless to enable me to command the full advantage of a more true and accurate aim.

A gentle breeze from the N.N.E. at last set in, to my unbounded satisfaction, which, by blowing off the land and from the craig, insures a space of very sheltered water at its base, and a tolerably smooth sea for many miles to the westward.

---

comparatively accessible; but this bird in Orkney, particularly if wanted in a hurry, is undeniably the most difficult to obtain.

On making my appearance, soon after breakfast, on the rough stone jetty, near the sloping foot of which the boat was moored, I at once perceived that Joseph had anticipated my feelings with praiseworthy ardour, as she evinced not only the still damp evidence of a thorough matutinal cleansing, but the yacht-like order of her tackle, and the care with which each rope or sail was coiled, stowed away, folded, or disposed for instant start, afforded silent but undoubted tokens of sailor-like neatness and attention. A moderate-sized deal box, which I had found most useful for containing the birds shot on my two previous expeditions, was again placed on board, together with waterproofs and overalls, not forgetting to fill the locker with all due comestibles, both edible and potatory. Mr. D——f again accompanied us, and as the inflated sail strained full upon the yard, the aroma of the fragrant and Virginian weed rose upon the gust that bore us from the quay.

I had taken care to provide myself with plenty of ammunition—shot, both large and small, wadding and patches, and sundry neat packages of Eley's cartridges were garnished with a goodly array of bright and fresh cast bullets. Both my gun and rifle were brought into requisition on this occasion, and the inspiriting adjuncts of a gloriously sunny and most lovely morning, while enhancing to the full the beaming smiles into which Nature was again so benignly melting, brightened on the sails of our tight little bark, and animated the buoyant aspirations of her jovial and high-spirited crew. All the early portion of the morning's sail was similar, so far as the land and sea objects were concerned, to that which I have described in my account of the voyage to Hoy. It took us a long but pleasant time tacking up the wind to reach a spot within a moderate walk by land, though we all felt that if the breeze continued it could not fail to bring us home apace.

The busy little puffins dived and sported on the distant wave, and the dark scarfes sped silently along. " A scene of more complete solitude, having all its peculiarities heightened by the extreme serenity of the weather, the quiet gray composed tone of the atmosphere, and the perfect silence of the elements, could hardly be imagined." The tide, although its upper surface was but little stirred by the action of the air, was running out with considerable rapidity and force; and the long and lessening waves, curling in their fall, chased each other with a fringing surge along the shelving sandy margin of the restless main.

Out upon a flat and awkward "skerrie," around which the waves were boiling and lashing with the expiring fury of a subsiding sea, and some distance off a turn of the land, rested a conclave of solemn shags; but it was not until they were well upon the wing, and too far off, that I perceived an eider duck amongst their number; while higher up upon this portion of the shore, were strewn and scattered many a fragment of hull and mast, the melancholy relics of a bygone wreck. As we rounded this spot (for we coasted the whole distance), the imposing object which we were now steadily approaching grew more defined upon the ravished sight with every ridge and furrow of the water through which we ploughed our way. And now this mighty monument of adamantine firmness, rigid and unmoved through countless ages, and witness of the ocean's most impetuous vagaries, rose, as it were, from the sea to the summit in one abrupt tremendous precipice.

There is something awe-inspiring to the very soul as you float in the vicinity of these dreadful spots; and, the more serene and undisturbed is the condition of the sea and air, the more potently you feel the loneliness and grandeur of their majestic desolation.

The aspect of this stupendous mass of rock, as from our fragile boat I gazed upon its rugged face, stretching away on either hand in one vast precipitous wall, was so severely grand and imposing that I feel the task of conveying to another mind a due and correct idea of the reality will be as difficult as it is impossible that I can ever, for my own part, cease to remember the sublimity of the scene. Magnificent, indeed, as viewed on this occasion from the fluctuating surface of a gently-heaving sea; but realise the same when reverberating with the full sway of ocean's wild commotion, and Schiller's beautiful words will seem adapted to this particular spot:

> "It hisses and eddies, and seethes and starts,
>   As if water and fire were blending,
> Till the spray-dashing column to heaven updarts,
>   Wave after wave everlastingly sending;
> Never exhausted and never at rest,
> Like a new sea sprung from the old sea's breast."

All the lowest strata, just as at Hoy Head, presented one overpowering scene of stirring active life, as every chink and inequality, the dark recesses of its dank and humid caverns, and every rugged flag or sloping block, was tenanted in a similar manner by thousands of the smaller sea-fowl. Many a noisy gull wheeled and screamed in mazy evolutions overhead, or floated in profound tranquillity upon the silent water. The large area of alternate wet and dry rock, giving birth, both upon its naked face and within its darksome fissures, to a luxuriant sea-growth of moist and reeking weed, imparted an odour of almost fetid saltness to the neighbouring air.

Upon the very topmost ridges the naked eye could just make out the breeding-places of the herring gull, which I have previously described; while stretching away on either side in one long line at one particular level, were two or three ledges in close proximity, on which the weird spectre-looking cormorants were standing, flying from, or returning, and some of the females sitting hard upon their nests. It was some time before I could clearly distinguish these curious birds amid the surrounding "minutiæ;" but, after a leisurely inspection, they became more familiar to my eye. The various prominences of one particular stratum were the sole and only places upon the face of this vast elevation that were frequented by the cormorant. From 140 to 170 yards off, they seemed quite near the summit of the craig; though from the upmost verge, I am told, they would appear as far below as they now were distant to the straining sight.

Many a shot re-echoed from my pieces, provoking the most deafening clamour, and my presence evidently created a "sensation." Not a bird, however, could I touch; nor did the continuous discharges tend in any serious way to disconcert them, as some sat close and motionless upon their hollow nests, and others stood at various points like gaunt revengeful fiends: "their slouching forms, their wet and vapid wings dangling from their sides to catch the breeze; while their weird, haggard, wildly-staring, emerald green eyes scowled about in all directions."

They must have commanded a gloriously-extensive view of the wilderness of waters, their wondrous storehouse and field of labour spreading into distance like a glistening carpet, as they eyed their mates so lovingly engaged, or watched their comrades rising like Longfellow's seaweed,

> "From the tumbling surf, that buries
> The Orkneyan skerries,
> Answering the hoarse Hebrides:
> And from wrecks of ships, and drifting
> Spars, uplifting
> On the desolate, rainy seas."

"These poor birds suffer severely when, during and after a continued gale, the Atlantic rolls in its enormous billows, dashing them against the headlands, and scouring with their fury the sounds and creeks. As far as the eye can reach, the ocean boils and heaves, presenting one boundless field of foam, the spray from the summits of the waves sweeping along the waste like drifted snow: no sign of life is to be seen, save when a gull, labouring hard to bear itself up against the blast, hovers overhead, or darts by like a meteor. If, at such a season, the haunts of the cormorants are visited, they will be found huddled together in their caves and crevices, perishing with hunger, and their numbers daily thinning by death. If, indeed, they could venture out, and bear the buffeting of the storm, they would still fail in procuring food; for as, in fishing, these birds always carry their heads under water, in order that, with their keen, clear, and beautiful eye, they may discover their prey at a greater distance, it is obvious that, in such commotions of the air and water, they would need even a quicker glance than they possess."

Perched at that amazing altitude, they seemed like gloomy sentinels placed to keep guard upon the lofty ramparts of one of Nature's strongholds. Dull and listless, there they sat, heedless of the warfare from below, calmly reviewing from their airy citadel, my puny efforts for their destruction.

Carefully reconnoitring every still and moving object throughout this world of life, I at last perceived one of these birds resting statue-like upon a sort of bracket-shaped protuberance, some thirty yards below the more thickly-inhabited ledge upon which the greater number of their nests were situated. He was, moreover, so ably protected from all danger by shot or bullet from below by the aforesaid projection, that, could I have brought my projectiles to bear upon the spot with any telling force and accuracy, the chances of injury to the bird itself were very slight indeed. The nature of the case accordingly suggested the following artifice, which I at once proceeded to carry out.

Handing the rifle to Joseph, and retaining the gun, both of whose barrels I had loaded with green cartridge, I requested him to fire first; and if he could not hit the bird, whose long pointed head and beak were alone visible, at all events to strike the rock immediately below. This he did; and as the bullet struck and chipped the very parapet of the ledge itself, the bird, flurried as I had hoped would be the case by this sudden and unexpected act of molestation, dropped from the ledge too suddenly to avail itself of that leverage or lifting power which the action of the legs affords to a bird when calmly rising from a stationary position, and sank a considerable distance before it was able to mount or feel at home upon the wing. It was just at this upward bend of its flight that I fired, and so effectually did the shot tell, that down came my bulky friend with a whiz and a speed that would have been attended with additional disaster had he dropped upon the heads of any of us, and, just clearing the boat, fell plump into the liquid sea, enveloping us, as he vanished, in a cloud of spray. After a few seconds he rose to the surface, and I bagged my first cormorant. We now rowed along the cliff for some distance each way, and I fired some fifteen or twenty shots in succession, without the least effect, the shot striking and glancing off their feathers like so much sand as they crossed and recrossed above my head, flying to and from the ledge.

I am strongly inclined to think that, in many instances, the cartridges "balled"—that is to say, they retained their solid form, without permitting the shot to spread—a fault which is not uncommon; and as I generally shot well ahead of my bird, by reason of the distance, they must have cleared him in a harmless manner. Joseph tells me that, on one occasion, when shooting at a greater black-backed gull, the cartridge so completely " balled " as to cause a large perforation entirely through the body of the bird.

In its fully-developed plumage, an old or adult cormorant possesses a beautiful white thigh or tibial feather, and I naturally spared no pains to obtain one with this appendage.

I was almost ceasing in despair, when one of my shots told at an immense distance, breaking the large joint of the wing, and the ponderous fellow, spinning round and round, descended with a fearful velocity, and as with a shout from the boat he entered the deep water with a plunge, a fan-shaped mist ascended, and then, after a few seconds had elapsed, he rose like a log to the surface. I stepped out and clambered on to the rough sloping back of an enormous insulated boulder, on which many a noble ship has ere this " come to grief," covered on every side with a rank and slippery growth of pendulous sea-weed, interspersed with millions of limpets, and around which the gentle swell was rising and falling, and, upon this, as inclining from the craig, I lay flat upon my face. Then, using its topmost edge as a rest for my rifle, I in this manner fired some twenty balls, most of them at one particular bird. Her head and upper portion of the neck I could alone perceive. She shook or drew back every now and then, as the bullets struck the rock behind her, but rested continuously upon her nest.

Finding this style of action of no avail, I returned to the boat, and after expending several more cartridges without effect, we rowed to a sort of natural pier of rock abutting upon a deep cavernous gorge containing the hollow which had been the means of preservation to the shipwrecked sailor, and I landed upon a broad sloping shelf, near to which I experienced a fall upon my last excursion to this cliff by land. Knowing that rock-pigeons build in the crannies overhead, I waited for a flight, and killed four young birds with my first two shots. A female rock pipit also fell to my share, ere I re-embarked. We now hoisted sail and stood off the land. The wind, together with the sea, was fast rising, many a " white nose " chequering the blueness of the more open water.

We bore almost across to Hoy before we put the helm down for the port tack ; and as the Kirk skerrie came in sight the glass showed me about a dozen shags, with one tall cormorant towering in the midst of them, drying their feathers in the breeze. The ring of the mainsail creaked upon the mast, which bent with each capricious gust ; and when within little less than a hundred yards, expecting every instant to see them rise, I whispered—" Shall I fire ?"

" We dare not approach any closer," replied Joseph, in a low tone, " on account of the shoal water, and must now stand off." Upon which I raised the gun, aimed high, held my breath, and pressed the trigger with all the steadiness I could command. To my exquisite joy and the delight of all, we noticed, as the greater number of the birds dispersed, that the cormorant and three of the shags were severely hit, and remained floating and diving around the skerrie. The difficulty was to get at them, and our only plan was to steer past the spot for some three-quarters of a mile to leeward, and then, returning on the other tack, to cut them off from the rock as they drifted with the tide. In this we were perfectly successful, thanks to Joseph's skilful hand, and the return sail was intensely exciting, as we could just descry the birds, unable to fly, but diving and swimming for very life. On coming up, we found the cormorant uncommonly strong and active (the shags having sufficiently recovered to escape), bearing well away, and struggling with the breakers to the westward.

Still nearer, an anxious chase at last gave me an opportunity for a second shot, which raised a very fountain from the wave, and stretched the bird effortless thereon. He proved to be a magnificient specimen, in fine full plumage, and weighed just $8\frac{1}{2}$ lbs. They are perfect pelicans in their way: the craw or gizzard is exceedingly elastic, and will expand to an immense extent; and they are unable to swallow and carry a vast weight of fish at one time. The peculiarity in the structure of the foot of this bird is remarkable; " the tarsi are stronger and more tendonous than in swimming-birds; they are straighter set, the toes collapse more, and thus the birds can walk better, and can also stand firm on the slippery points of rocks." The web, also, is continued to the hind toe; the general position of the same being inwards rather than forwards. Mr. Scarth tells me "that he has tasted cormorant soup, and that its flavour much resembles that of hare." It being now evident that a gale was setting in, we took advantage of the same, and, running briskly up the tideway, returned to Stromness by the hour of five. A hazy gloom o'erspread the darkening sky, and the day which had begun so brightly ended in a drizzling rain; and the angry sea, ever changeful as the life of man, broke upon the distant headlands with the roar of thunder.

CHAPTER IX.

"Encourag'd thus, she brought her younglings nigh,
Watching the motions of her patron's eye,
*   *   *   *   ; the rest amaz'd,
Stood mutely still and on the stranger gazed.
DRYDEN.

"It was the owl that shriek'd, the fatal bellman, which gives the stern'st good night."—SHAKSPEARE.

IT was a fair bright morning in June (the 19th). The cool soft breeze that floated in from the seaward played around my temples with a delicious freshness, as I loaded my gun with large and small shot, and cautiously set to work beneath the shade of a long range of hills. The ground varies exceedingly about this part of the Mainland. Now, a spreading extent of peat bog; now, a considerable patch of dry bleached heather; now, a carpet of rich green moss; now, a puny jungle of dying reeds and rushes. Relying upon undoubted intelligence that short-eared owls and other rare birds, rapidly becoming still more scarce, have been known to breed about these parts, I determined to make the utmost of the locality, and to use my best endeavours to discover the whereabouts, and, if possible, to secure a specimen of one or other of the same. Surveying and reconnoitring the ground, I singled out a limited extent of country, and beat it steadily to an inch, as though it contained but a single living animal. If stiff knee-deep heather, then my progress was slow, as I cautiously raised every likely tuft with my foot or the muzzle of my gun, or peered within its mossy depths with curious suspicion.

I had not proceeded far before a very unusual note higher up the hill smote my ear, and, in a few more steps, the bird rose and fell to my shot, a fine snipe in rich summer plumage. In about a quarter of an hour later I came upon the fragments of the egg-shells of the common wild duck, and, stooping down, I found the nest rifled and torn, doubtless by those villainous and unsparing robbers, the corbies or hooded crows. Some time afterwards, amid the interstices of the dry moss upon a little hillock, I discovered the bleached skulls of the young of the shorteared owl (*Strix brachyotus*). In another spot, well concealed by dense vegetation, an old last-year's nest still existed, but I am unable to state to what bird it could have belonged. Quantities of the large, hairy caterpillar (*Caja*) appeared in all directions upon the ground foliage, no doubt simultaneously brought into existence by a recent warm change. I sprang another snipe out of distance, and then continued carefully on, quartering the ground without the faintest glimpse of the bird it now became my great ambition to descry. After two hours' further hard walking, I had beaten a very considerable tract of the hill-side, and nothing living seemed to animate the scene, save a few pairs of the universal peewit, a solitary wheatear, or the common brown linnet, one of whose snug little nests I almost trod upon.

The sun was shining with power—not a breath of wind was stirring—the face of nature was serene, and, feeling slightly exhausted with exertion, I threw myself upon the heather, and revelled in the picture stretching gaily from below. Extended at my feet, and sweeping as far as the eye could reach, lay the beautiful Bay of Firth—its waters calm and placid as a mill-pond, and its outline and its surface picturesquely broken by numberless small islands, the feeding spots of cattle, and the breeding haunts of gulls. A sort of dreamy doze is half engendered by the serenity of such a scene. Relapsing slowly into this condition, a faint and distant cry, resembling a female hysterical laugh, assailed my startled ear. Straining in the direction from which it had proceeded, I quickly espied a large bird of the hawk kind hovering over the summit of the hill above my right; at one moment just about to soar, then sinking in its flight and gliding along the brow, it seemed evidently half inclined to settle on the heather—now steadily sustaining itself over some attractive spot, and at intervals reiterating the cry I have endeavoured to describe above.

Conscious of the wary nature of these birds, still and solid as a rock I lay, intently watching, as a wrecker might be supposed to do, the shifts and writhings of a doomed vessel approaching inevitable destruction. After a few uncertain circlings, it evidently settled beyond a little piece of rising ground. Instantly divesting myself of unnecessary weight, I hurried to the spot. When about half-way thither, the bird rose as I expected, but made towards me, rising higher on the wing at every stroke. When within range I fired and killed, to my no small satisfaction, a magnificent female hen harrier (*Falco cyaneus*). Returning for my collecting-box (no cenotaph to-day! thought I), I was in the act of consigning her to its depths, when that cry, shriller and more sustained, heralded the male bird making his appearance from the same direction. I studiously recommenced the stalk, but this time my position was more exposed, and it was impossible to improve it without a very prominent and injudicious *détour*. My only chance consisted in remaining perfectly still in the position I then was. This I did, and I watched *him*, and doubtless he watched *me* with still greater vigilance and caution.

It now became most deeply interesting to watch his plan of operations. At one time soaring to a dizzy height; then scouring in wider circles the adjacent valley; again, flying steadily up hill, hunting every yard of ground and sailing parallel to the ascent, he repeated his cry more plaintively at shorter intervals, and was evidently perplexed and dismayed at receiving no acknowledgment or reply from his now defunct spouse. I at once felt quite decided that their nest must exist somewhere upon the border of the brae. Revolving in my brain the proceedings of the last few minutes, I determined to reconnoitre the ground where I last observed the female bird had chosen to alight. While in the act of making to the spot a snake-like hissing sound arrested my further progress, and, looking down in tremulous uncertainty, a perfect picture, so to speak, transfixed me with delight.

Elegantly grouped, with wings extended and eyelets flashing with the fire of frightened scorn, like infantine avenging satyrs guarding the person of the young Endymion, four young birds, almost able to fly, of various ages and consequent stages of imperfect plumage, with one addled egg, rested upon the level platform of their rush-built nest. After the excitement of the preceding moments, and absorbed with the effective picturesqueness of the sight, I gazed with something of that trance of pleasure which would undoubtedly have swayed a painter's breast.

The male bird, unable any longer to control his emotions, now approached within range, and feeling that I had already commenced a work of destruction that completeness alone could excuse, I fired, and with a bump upon the ground, he fell perpendicularly to my shot. With the impression that I had unmistakably disposed of him, I lowered my gun, when, to my astonishment, he rose again apparently uninjured, and sped away steadily and strong along the distance-melting defiles of the vale. Swallowing the disappointment as best I could, I then as humanely as possible consigned the youthful members of the family to a premature decease. On the first introduction of my hand, however, so virulent was the attack of two of these fledglings in their defensive pounce, as literally to leave their talons in my glove, completely dissevered from their tender feet. Having stowed them carefully in my collecting-box, and feeling exceedingly annoyed at my unanticipated loss of the male bird, which, without a shadow of a doubt, could not long have survived the effects of the shot, and must have been at this moment lying dead at some point of the vale below, I made a wide *détour* in the direction of its flight, most carefully beating every portion of the ground. It, however, availed me nothing, and I wended my way to Bin' Scarth steadily and without delay.

Early on the ensuing morning—which was ushered in with a drizzling mist, suggesting visions of sea-trout rising eagerly at the mouth of the loch—I again set forth, pregnant with hope, to scour a greater stretch of the hill-side, and extend my peregrinations, if time allowed, along the undulating ridges of the Braes of Harray.

Having gained the scene of the previous day's success, I at once struck off towards a higher elevation of the mountain, and making up to a solitary cow-herd, questioned him minutely as to whether any birds of prey—but more especially owls—had come within his recent observation. To all my queries he returned a vacant negative; but having heard from other sources that these birds are known from time to time to frequent and hunt about this portion of the island, and are occasionally to be found resting lazily upon the fern, I pursued my way undiscouraged, and determined to work to the utmost every likely-looking piece of ground within a somewhat undefined but widely-extended beat. Crossing the topmost ridge, and on the point of descending the opposite slope, I halted, in order to distinguish and make choice of those places where the heather flourished with the greatest luxuriance, or wherever a patch of bracken, sheltered by the rising ground from the ravages of the devastating sea-blast, gave token of more advanced growth, and waved its fresh young fronds obedient to the gentlest gust. I here bagged a lovely specimen of the golden plover, my attention being attracted to it by the singular beauty and distinctness of its breast plumage; a broad irregular streak of a rich black hue, and characteristic of the full maturity of its summer dress, being continued down the centre of the same. Pressing onwards, with measured stride, for nearly four hours, and discovering no clue or trace of the existence of these birds, I decided to confine my attentions to higher ground, and accordingly commenced the ascent of a considerable hill to my right. Much of the ground I had just traversed was perfectly "honeycombed" with rabbit-holes, over which the heather had grown so thickly that they were completely screened from sight, and the footing was thereby rendered precarious and difficult. I sprang several snipe on the lower ground, but could not succeed in discovering the slightest indications of their nests. After another half-hour's hard walking, my endeavours being still fruitless as to the object of my search, I was suddenly startled from a short reverie into which I had fallen by the barking of a "colley" dog, quickly followed by the animal itself irate and noisy. Looking about me for his master, I perceived two boys herding sheep upon the brow above, one of whom informed me that he knew of a nest some distance off on the eastern side of the hill. Persuading him to accompany me, we pushed on for another three-quarters of a mile down the eastward slope, until, on approaching a spot where the ground assumed a more peaty nature, and was watered by a gushing spring, one of the long-sought birds rose from the fern ; but, in my excitement, I fired a little too soon, and it fell (a female) rather severely shattered by the charge. Close by, and snugly shaded by the branching fern, lay her flat but slightly-hollowed nest, built of dead sticks and dry coarse-grass, and containing five eggs.* I saw no appearance of the male bird, though I watched and waited some time. I now elicited from my guide that another of these birds continually haunted the neighbourhood of a burn, about a mile to the southward. I at once set off enlivened with success, and, as we approached the course of the said rivulet, the worn and sunken bed of which, walled in, as it were, by its precipitous banks, was almost screened from view by the luxuriance of the heather on either side, an exclamation from the herd-boy arrested my attention, as he pointed to a small black speck, a long distance ahead, circling and hunting about in a hawk-like manner. "There he is, sir!" he remarked; and I paused a considerable time to enjoy the interesting spectacle of a bird of the owl kind busily engaged in seeking its prey in the broad bright daylight.

Crouching low in the bosky heather, I waited in delusive expectation that in one of his widening and varied flights he would approach within shot. This manœuvre proved of no service, and as I soon perceived that his evolutions were confined to a limited area, I

* " The eggs of this bird," says Yarrell, "seldom exceed three in number."

at once concluded that the nest, and perchance his mate (supposing this to be the male bird), would be found somewhere within the same boundary. I now, therefore, rose and walked steadily up to the spot, the bird either rising higher on the wing, or perching at intervals upon the heather. He allowed me to approach sufficiently close to fire, but before I did so I stumbled upon the nest containing, or rather upon which stood, the female bird and four young ones. This was a gratifying discovery after my long ramble, and the spectacle was immensely enhanced by another circumstance which illustrated the providence and care of the parent birds in a most interesting manner. Neatly disposed at equidistant points around the margin of the nest, which resembled a flat circular dish daintily garnished for the table, lay the result of the male bird's foraging activity in the shape of two large field mice and a young linnet. The young birds were about half-fledged, and in another fortnight would have been able to shift for themselves. In addition to them I succeeded in securing both the parent birds in excellent condition. Mr. Broderip, in his 'Zoological Recreations,' says that "this owl, though found breeding in these parts, regularly migrates to our island, from the north, about October ; and in consequence of the general arrival of these birds in the southern parts of Britain with the first fair October winds, they are called woodcock owls, an appellation branded on the memory of more than one luckless would-be-sportsman."

From some turnip-field hard by a plantation, or a tuft of rushes close to a copse on a moist hill-side, up springs a russet-plumaged bird, and is in the covert in a moment.

The eager shooter " catches a glintse on 'in," as an old keeper used to say, through the trees. Bang goes the gun. "That's the first cock of the season!" exclaims he, exultingly.

Up comes John, who has been sent ostensibly to attend him, but really to take care of him.

"I'm sure he's down," pointing to the covert—as many are apt to say when they shoot at a cock without being able to produce the body.

"Well, let's look, sir. Where did a' drop?" "There, just by that holly." In they go, retriever and all.

"There he lies," cries the delighted shot, loading his gun triumphantly in measureless content, "dead as Harry the Eighth. I knew he was down—there—just where I said he was, close by that mossy stump. Can't you see?"

"Iss, sir, I sees well enough, but I don't like the looks on 'in; his head's a trifle too big, and a' do lie too flat on his face."

"Pick up the cock, I say," rejoins our hero, somewhat nettled.

"I can't do that, sir," says John, lifting up a fine

specimen of *Otus palustris*, and holding it up to the blank-looking cockney, amid the ill-suppressed laughter of those confounded fellows who attend to mark not only the game, but the number of shots that are missed, on their abominable knotched sticks.

"Never mind, sir," adds the comforter John, "if t'ant a cock, a' did keep company wi' 'em; and a's curious like, and since you ha'nt killed nothen else to-day, I'd bag un if I was you—he'll look uncommon well in a glass case."

On my way home I passed another of these birds hunting about in their slow and noiseless manner.

CHAPTER X.

> " At morn the blackcock trims his jetty wing,
>   'Tis morning prompts the linnet's blithest lay,
> All nature's children feel the matin spring
>   Of life reviving, with reviving day;
> And while yon little bark glides down the bay,
> Wafting the stranger on his way again,
> Morn's genial influence roused a minstrel grey."

It was the dawn of early morning as I once more stept on board the little steam-packet to take my final departure; the waters of the bay were as smooth as glass; steaming mists hung round the summit of Hoy and the adjoining rocks, and I felt that summer was at hand.

The plan of my future movements has, for the last few days, been somewhat undecided, for I had hoped to have extended my tour to the Shetland Isles; but, having been so far successful in securing specimens of the common varieties among the fauna of our northern shores, I have decided to " cease firing," and peaceably to direct my steps southwards, in the anticipation of accomplishing a visit to these islands, in conjunction with a voyage to Iceland, at an earlier season of a future year. I have been disappointed in obtaining some few species, such as the common skua (*Lestris catarractus*) and the Fulmar petrel (*Procellaria glacialis*), which I had good reason to believe might have been found breeding in some of the localities I have mentioned; to say nothing of our more rare and occasional visitants among the *Laridæ*, as the ivory or Iceland gulls, &c. I can, however, most truly aver that this, my first essay to become more intimately acquainted with my feathered companions, has been replete with the utmost enjoyment, by introducing to my notice and appreciation the more rugged beauties of our North British scenery in some of its wildest and most unfrequented spots. It was therefore with no small reluctance, that, bidding adieu to the Orcadian group, I returned to Thurso on the morning of the 28th of June, and proceeded thence by the Hamburg steamer to Aberdeen. I there took the train to the fair city of Perth; and, as I leant upon the parapet of its bridge, in the quietude of a still warm evening, and surveyed the noble Tay rolling majestically below, its innumerable ripples sparkling with a thousand hues along its pebbly bed, the contrast between the prose of the bleaker north and the more poetical luxuriance of the present scene was inexpressibly alluring. I here noticed my old friends the blackheaded gulls, their breeding duties probably ended, sailing about with outstretched wings in the most fearless and unsuspecting manner.

The effect of the surrounding prospect, embracing the distant Grampians, backed by the expansive green sward of the North Inch, the scene of the battle in "The Fair Maid," and enhanced by my having the good fortune to behold it in the midst of the transient loveliness of the opening summer, tempted me to pause in my route; to woo fair Nature in her richer garb; to wander over foss and fell; and to loiter for awhile amid the sylvian and aquatic beauties of the Trossachs. It was during my stay at Callander that I found the common curlew (*Numenius arquata*), breeding in the rising hay grass on the banks of the Teith, and a pair of them were kindly shot for me by the keeper of Holt Skinner, Esq. Perhaps at no time does the enchantment of romantic scenery adapt itself to the imagination with more thrilling force than as in the present instance; and after my recent experience of a country strangely denuded of trees, even to the smallest bush, I found myself strolling, fly rod in hand, amidst the loveliest recesses of the same, heightened by the combined effects of peculiarly brilliant weather, and the fresh pale emerald-green of the bursting foliage. The calm serenity of lake and dell, and the mingled voices of the smaller song birds from the leafy boughs, was a relief to my soul after the treeless wastes amid the roar of ocean.

> " The summer dawn's reflected hue
> To purple changed Loch Katrine blue;
> Mildly and soft the western breeze
> Just kissed the lake, just stirred the trees—"

would have been a very inappropriate description on the occasion of my visit, being lashed by a stiff south-easter into the wildest commotion; so that even a moderately heavy " tub," with two sturdy boatmen at the oars, which myself and a friend had engaged for the day, was tossed about in a very unceremonious manner. Notwithstanding these adverse circumstances we were successful in luring thirteen nice trout from its depths, extremely dark in colour, though their flesh cut beautifully red when brought to table. On the four following days the sun burst forth with an intensity singularly unfavourable to piscatorial enterprise. Nevertheless I did not desert my colours, and Loch Vennachar and Loch Lubnaig received their due share of my attentions. The latter is a long winding loch, in the midst of some wild and bold scenery; the sides of the hills, that slope to the water's brink, being much less wooded than those in the more immediate vicinity of the Trossachs.

We commenced betimes at the mouth of this loch on the morning of the 4th, after a four mile walk; but the trout were disinclined to rise, and the extreme smoothness of the water, the denseness of the fog, and the stillness of the atmosphere, presaged a broiling day.

> "The grey mist left the mountain side,
> The torrent showed its glistening pride;
> Invisible in fleckèd sky
> The lark sent down her revelry;
> The blackbird and the speckled thrush
> Good morrow gave from brake and brush;
> In answer cooed the cushat dove
> Her notes of peace, and rest, and love."

Many salmon find their way into this loch every "spate;" but though we spun the parr-tail assiduously we did not succeed in moving one. We killed twenty-one trout, but the day was too sultry to expect sport. As I reclined upon the scorching seats of the boat I noticed the common wild duck and the little grebe breeding amongst the sedges, while the clefts and fissures of the mountain sides were a very paradise for the raven (*Corvus corax*), a pair of which ill-omened bird I succeeded in obtaining, as well as that dapper little itinerant whistler the common sandpiper (*Totanus hypoleucos*). A precipitous and imposing craig jutting from the bosom of Ben Ledi, and overshadowing the darkest and deepest portion of the lake, has long been tenanted by a pair of golden eagles (*Falco chrysaëtos*), and I gazed with a species of rapture upon their well-chosen and inaccessible eyrie, placed upon the very summit of its "thunder-splintered pinnacle."

It was on an occasion such as this that even my fisherman's patience became exhausted, and being desirous of diversifying the day's proceedings, I set to work to ascend the hill immediately above me. The slope was seriously steep, and wet and slippery under foot. Having made about two-thirds of its height, the rumble of a rivulet under my feet almost prevented my hearing the cry of a buzzard above me. The note of this bird is so peculiar, that I thought of the words quoted by Scott in " Waverley " :

> " She shudders and stops as the charm she speaks :
> Is it the moody owl that shrieks?
> Or is it that sound betwixt laughter and scream,
> The voice of the demon who haunts the stream?
> *St. Swithin's Chair.*

I could not, however, discern the bird. Stimulated thereby I doubled my exertions, and, having gained another ledge, I looked up, and perceived a magnificent specimen on the wing, though he quickly settled on a point of the craig above my head. I soon made a slight *détour*, with the intention of stalking him. The last part of the acclivity was very steep, but I reached the summit, and was creeping on to the ledge above him, when he again took wing out of gunshot, and circled imposingly over the very lake itself. His distant cry now died away, and I lost sight of him for ever. Terribly out of breath, I rested upon a piece of rock jutting out invitingly from the grassy steep, and as welcome to my weary muscles as the water-plant to the thirsty African. The scene that met my gaze was magnificent in the extreme. The unsullied loch (from a narrow arm of which a small river—a tributary of the Clyde—swept onwards towards the same) lay like a sheet of looking-glass below; while the radiant sky, the reflections in the water, the universal silence, were so charming in effect, that I may be excused if my thoughts there and then resolved themselves in the following form :

Majestically rolling the Highland rivers flow;
Their rippled bosoms courting the breezes as they blow:
While the bubble of the streamlet and the gurgle of the rill
Gently whisper back, mellifluous, the echo from the hill.

Onward ever nobly rushing, through the valley and the fell,
By the mountain and the moorland, through the dingle and the dell;
Their darker depths invite to lave and cleave the waters cool,
Where the swirling of the torrent breaks the eddy of the pool.

There's a quiet in the stilly air—a solitude, a rest,
As the fleeting shadows flit along the mountain's rugged breast;
While the brilliancy of sunlight with the sombreness of shade
Brighten up fair Nature's landscape and illuminate the glade.

Mark the fisher on the margin wield the pliant supple rod;
Direct the free and lithesome line upon the foaming flood,
To lure its finny denizens and draw them to the side—
The speckled trout and salmon, wily monarch of the tide.

Mirror'd in the limpid loch behold the azure sky;
The cloudlets sweep athwart it, and are caught reflectively;
And harmonious commingle with a rich and varied hue,
Heath and heather, russet bracken, and the moss-grown granite too.

With a happy thrill of freedom do I drink the bracing air;
I feel it in my life-blood as I mount the rugged stair;
And I envy still the skylark skyward singing as I roam,
Making music in the desert, in the wilderness a home.

FINIS.

E. NEWMAN, PRINTER, 9, DEVONSHIRE STREET, BISHOPSGATE, N.E.

INDISPENSABLE WORKS ON BRITISH BIRDS.

I.

THE ZOOLOGIST;
A Monthly Journal of Natural History,
FOR RECORDING FACTS AND ANECDOTES RELATING TO QUADRUPEDS, BIRDS, REPTILES, FISHES AND INSECTS.

Conducted by EDWARD NEWMAN, F.L.S., F.Z.S., &c.

The Editor has been assisted by more than two hundred of our best Zoologists, among whom are the following:—

C. C. Babington, M.A., F.L.S.
Dr. Baird, F.L.S.
H. W. Bates
Prof. Bell, F.L.S.
T. J. Bold, of Newcastle
Frederick Bond
C. R. Bree, M.D.
Lord Clermont
Lord Clifton
John Cordeaux
Thomas Cornish
Rev. H. Harpur Crewe, M.A.
Jonathan Couch, F.L.S.
R. Q. Couch, of Penzance
J. C. Dale, F.L.S.
Henry Doubleday
J. W. Douglas
Thomas Edward, of Banff
Dr. J. E. Gray, F.R.S.
G. R. Gray, F.L.S.
Rev. Joseph Greene, M.A.
J. H. Gurney
Rev. Dr. Gordon, M.A.
P. H. Gosse, F.R.S.
Captain Hadfield
J. E. Harting, F.Z.S.

W. C. Hewitson
Harry Blake-Knox
Sir W. M. E. Milner, Bart.
Sir Oswald Mosley, Bart.
Alfred Newton, M.A.
Rev. A. Merle Norman, M.A.
John Rocke
Edward Hearle Rodd
Howard Saunders, F.Z.S.
W. W. Saunders, F.R.S., &c.
H. L. Saxby, M.D.
P. L Sclater, Ph.D., F.Z.S.
Dr. Berthold Seeman
Rev. Alfred C. Smith, M.A.
H. T. Stainton, F.L.S.
Stephen Stone, F.L.S.
Samuel Stevens, F.L.S.
Henry Stevenson
R. Swinhoe, F.Z.S., F.G.S., &c.
A. R. Wallace, F.L.S.
George R. Waterhouse, F.Z.S.
The late Charles Waterton
Prof. Westwood, F.L.S.
Sir Gardner Wilkinson
T. V. Wollaston, M.A., F.L.S.
The late W. Yarrell, F.L.S.

⁂ Monthly Notes on British Birds from all parts of the United Kingdom.

PRICE 12s. A-YEAR, POST FREE.

☞ *A New Series was commenced in* 1866.

JOHN VAN VOORST, 1, PATERNOSTER ROW.

INDISPENSABLE WORKS ON BRITISH BIRDS.

II.
A DICTIONARY OF BRITISH BIRDS.
By EDWARD NEWMAN, F.L.S., F.Z.S., &c.

EDITOR OF THE 'ZOOLOGIST' AND 'ENTOMOLOGIST.'

1. In this work the whole of Colonel Montagu's 'Dictionary,' 'Supplement' and 'Appendix,' are reprinted in a combined and alphabetical order, the words SUPPLEMENT and APPENDIX being prefixed to whatever is derived from these two sources. Nothing that Montagu has published is omitted or altered.

2. Observation and discovery are incessantly at work: it is no more possible for our knowledge to remain stationary than for this earth to discontinue its rotation; hence the additions which Colonel Montagu found it necessary to make between 1802, the date of the 'Dictionary,' and 1813, the date of the Supplement: these additions, now incorporated, exceed the original work in bulk. In 1833 Mr. Selby published his 'Illustrations of British Ornithology,' and in this work twenty-four species unknown to Colonel Montagu were described. In 1843 Mr. Yarrell published the first edition of his 'History of British Birds;' in 1846 a second edition, and in 1856 a third and final edition: in these three editions that amiable and most painstaking author added, from various sources, no less than fifty-nine species. The 'Zoologist' has added twenty-one species to those mentioned by Montagu, Selby and Yarrell. The descriptions of these added species are extracted from the works of Temminck, Selby and Yarrell, are marked by inverted commas, and accompanied by a reference to the volume and page.

3. Immediately after the name is inserted a reference to a figure of the *bird* and a figure of the *egg*: these references are added both to the original and the new descriptions. For this purpose Yarrell's 'History of British Birds' and Hewitson's 'Oology' have been selected: these works are at present, and for the next half-century will certainly continue, our standard authorities: these interpolations are also enclosed in editorial brackets.

PRICE TWELVE SHILLINGS.

JOHN VAN VOORST, 1, PATERNOSTER ROW.

INDISPENSABLE WORKS ON BRITISH BIRDS.

III.

BIRDSNESTING;

Being a complete Description of the Nests and Eggs of Birds which breed in Great Britain and Ireland.

By EDWARD NEWMAN, F.L.S., F.Z.S., &c.

This work is written expressly for the use of out-of-door naturalists and that better class of schoolboys who take up Natural History as an instructive recreation. Under each species will be found—

1. The English name.
2. The Latin name.
3. The situation in which the nest is to be found.
4. The materials of which the nest is built, together with any particulars of its shape which may assist in determining by what bird it is built.
5. The number and colour of the eggs, describing such variations as are occasionally met with.

In compiling this work the sources whence the author has drawn his information are—

1. His own memoranda.
2. Colonel Montagu's 'Ornithological Dictionary.'
3. Mr. Selby's 'Illustrations of British Ornithology.'
4. Mr. Hewitson's 'Oology.'
5. The 'Zoologist,' not only every volume but every number of which abounds in original and highly important observations on the life-history and distinguishing characters of birds.
6. The "Letters of Rusticus."
7. Observations, emendations and additions, by Mr. Bond, of London, and Mr. Doubleday, of Epping.

PRICE ONE SHILLING.

JOHN VAN VOORST, 1, PATERNOSTER ROW.

INDISPENSABLE WORKS ON BRITISH BIRDS.

IV.

SUGGESTIONS

FOR FORMING

COLLECTIONS OF BIRDS' EGGS.

By ALFRED NEWTON, Esq., M.A.

These 'Suggestions' are from the pen of Mr. Newton, than whom no one was ever better qualified for the task. The first object is to identify the egg, to be quite sure to what bird it belongs. Mr. Newton justly considers that an egg wrongly named is worse than no specimen at all. As soon as the egg is positively identified, the next object is to authenticate it, by attaching such a mark as can neither be removed nor obliterated. Then follows a full and most minute description of the mode of blowing eggs : it is expressly explained that no hole should be visible, and it is also explained how to avoid this; on no account whatever should there be a hole at either end, and there should be but one hole. The difficulty of removing the contents from eggs that have been sat on and nearly hatched is entirely overcome; and the proper instruments to use are not only described but figured, and the requisite information is given where they may be obtained. Finally, we are shown how to strengthen the shell of delicate eggs before drilling the hole through which their contents are to be emptied.

PRICE SEVENPENCE, POST FREE.

V.

THE ZOOLOGIST LIST of BRITISH BIRDS, compiled from Mr. Yarrell's standard work on British Birds, comprising all the additions and corrections necessary up to July, 1866. Price, printed on both sides, 3d., post free; or on one side only, for Labels, 5d., post free.

JOHN VAN VOORST, 1, PATERNOSTER ROW.

VI.
A HISTORY OF BRITISH FERNS.
By EDWARD NEWMAN, F.L.S., F.Z.S.

This work is illustrated by One Hundred Engravings, which are carefully executed by some of our first artists, from the Author's own drawings on the wood, and consist of studiously accurate Figures of every Species and Variety of Fern found in Great Britain. Under each species there is also a most minute Description and ample List of Localities, and full Directions for Cultivating. This work is the result of many years of unremitting labour, and of frequent journeys on foot in various parts of England, Wales, Scotland and Ireland, undertaken by the Author with the view of observing, in their natural stations, the plants he has described.

OPINIONS OF THE PRESS.

"It is a great gratification to have it in our power most cordially to recommend this work to all those who desire to obtain a knowledge of our British Ferns, as one which in accuracy of observation, elaborateness and clearness of description, and beauty of illustration, does not possess its equal."—*Professor Babington, in.' Annals of Natural History.'*

"It is just such books as this which render Natural History so attractive to everybody who finds other pleasures in a country life besides hunting, coursing, fishing and shooting."—*Professor Lindley, in 'Gardener's Chronicle.'*

"'Those who are desirous of acquiring an intimate acquaintance with our native species of this beautiful and interesting order of plants cannot do better than consult Mr. Newman's 'History of British Ferns.'"—*Mr. Ward, on the Growth of Plants in Closely Glazed Cases.*

THE ROYAL EDITION, 36s.   THE THIRD EDITION, 18s.
THE FOURTH OR SCHOOL EDITION, 5s.

JOHN VAN VOORST, 1, PATERNOSTER ROW.

INDISPENSABLE WORKS on BRITISH NATURAL HISTORY.

VII.
THE INSECT HUNTERS.
By EDWARD NEWMAN, F.L.S., F.Z.S.,
Late President of the Entomological Society.

I have written this little book expressly for those who do not pretend to consider themselves experienced naturalists. I do not assume any knowledge on the part of the learner, but begin at the beginning, and attempt to educate the reader up to the point of understanding my more complete and extended 'Familiar Introduction to the History of Insects;' indeed I am not altogether without a hope that some will consider this inexpensive and unassuming little book a sufficient introduction to the Science.—EDWARD NEWMAN.

"UNRIVALLED AS A FIRST-BOOK IN ENTOMOLOGY."—*The late William Spence, F.R.S., one of the Authors of the celebrated 'Introduction to Entomology.'*

"Undoubtedly the best and most useful of Mr. Newman's entomological works."—*H. T. Stainton, F.L.S., in 'Entomologist's Annual' for 1858.*

"There is a capital chapter on Metamorphosis, and the families in all the orders have their prominent characteristics concisely yet emphatically set forth. . . . . For the young who have not had their attention drawn to Entomology we think this an admirable book, one that a parent might give to his child without any fear that the contents were not strictly true."—*Entomologist's Weekly Intelligencer.*

PRICE TWO SHILLINGS AND SIXPENCE.

JOHN VAN VOORST, 1, PATERNOSTER ROW.

VIII.
NEWMAN'S 'ENTOMOLOGIST;'
A POPULAR MONTHLY JOURNAL OF BRITISH ENTOMOLOGY.

Published at Sixence each Number, or Six Shillings a-year, the *Postage prepaid.*

The Objects of the 'Entomologist' are :—

1st. To work out the Life-history of all Insects injurious to Agriculture and Horticulture; to suggest remedies for their ravages, and publish full details of successful experiments for their destruction.

2nd. To preserve a continuous record of captures in every part of the kingdom: the earliest possible notice of these is most earnestly requested.

3rd. To improve collections, more especially of British Lepidoptera, by the free communication of specimens; for this purpose all Lists of Duplicates and Desiderata are admitted without any charge.

4th. To give all Entomological News that can be considered of general interest, including Reports of Meetings.

IX.
SYNONYMIC LIST of BRITISH BUTTERFLIES AND MOTHS.
By Henry Doubleday, Esq. This is the only complete List of British Lepidopterous Insects. It contains the name and synonymes of every Butterfly and Moth discovered in Great Britain up to the end of 1865.—Price, printed on one side only for Labels, 1s. 6d., post free.

X.
A HISTORY OF BRITISH BUTTERFLIES.
By Edward Newman, F.L.S., F.Z.S. Contains a figure of every British Butterfly, exactly the size of life, and also a full description of each in the various stages of Caterpillar, Chrysalis and Butterfly, with all particulars of the plant on which the Caterpillar feeds, and *full instructions how to find, catch and preserve Butterflies and Moths.*—Price Sevenpence, post free.

E. NEWMAN, 9, DEVONSHIRE STREET, BISHOPSGATE.

BOTANICAL DRYING PAPER.

In soliciting the attention of Botanists to the above paper, Edward Newman begs to state it is manufactured expressly for the purpose of DRYING SPECIMENS FOR THE HERBARIUM. It possesses all the qualities required in such paper, preserving form and colour in the best possible manner, and having the peculiar advantage of seldom, if ever, requiring a change of sheets whilst the plants are being dried, a process by which much time is lost. Its stoutness and durability also combine to render it economical, making it *practically* quite as cheap as ordinary paper sold at a lower price. Edward Newman feels much pleasure in being able to state that its merits have been fully proved by our most eminent Botanists, extracts from some of whose valuable Testimonials in its favour are here subjoined.

"All I have to say is in its favour. It is the best paper for the purpose I have ever employed."—*The late Sir W. J. Hooker.*

"I have now made use of your paper during the whole of my summer tour in Scotland, and have found it to be by far the best paper for drying specimens of plants that I have ever used."—*Professor Babington.*

THE FOLLOWING ARE THE SIZES AND PRICES:—
16 inches by 10 when folded, 10d. ⍑ quire.
18 „ 11 „ 1s. „
20 „ 12 „ 1s. 4d. „
20 „ 16 „ 1s. 8d. „

☞ THIS PAPER IS TOO HEAVY TO SEND BY POST.

E. NEWMAN, 9, DEVONSHIRE STREET, BISHOPSGATE.

www.ingramcontent.com/pod-product-compliance
Lightning Source LLC
Chambersburg PA
CBHW030351170426
43202CB00010B/1338